Preaching Without Notes

Preaching Without Notes

Joseph M. Webb

ABINGDON PRESS
NASHVILLE

PREACHING WITHOUT NOTES

This book is printed on recycled, acid-free paper.

Library of Congress Cataloging-in-Publication Data

Webb, Joseph M., 1942-
  Preaching without notes / Joseph M. Webb.
      p.   cm.
  ISBN 0-687-09088-1 (alk. paper)
  1. Extemporaneous preaching.   I. Title.
BV4235.E8 W43 2001
251—dc21
                                                                    00-045128
ISBN 13: 978-0-687-09088-4

Scripture quotations, unless otherwise indicated, are from the New Revised
Standard Version Bible, copyright © 1989, by the Division of Christian
Education of the National Council of the Churches of Christ in the United
States of America.

09 10—10

MANUFACTURED IN THE UNITED STATES OF AMERICA

For Lindsay Elizabeth,
first grandchild,
born at the end of an old century,
growing to maturity in the new.
She entered life just as this book
was coming into being.

Contents

Preface

Not long ago, I visited a large metropolitan Protestant church in which a strange thing happened. At the appropriate point in the service, the pastor asked the children to come and gather around her on the chancel steps for their time together. Within a moment, she was surrounded as she sat among the children on the top step. For the next ten minutes or so she talked with them—effortlessly, naturally, with spontaneity and laughter, with down-to-earth insight and carefully prepared thought. The children were mesmerized. So were those of us who were listening to her from the pew. The things that she said were picturesque, easy to follow, and, in retrospect, very important. In what seemed like a flash, it was over. But it was an extraordinary moment. After a brief prayer, she dismissed the children, and the service went on.

A short time later, the same preacher stepped into the pulpit, arranged her manuscript in front of her, and, for the next twenty minutes, read it—meticulously, with as much enthusiasm as she could muster, particularly at the beginning, but with diminishing energy the farther she went. She tired of the reading, so listening was difficult, particularly toward the end, even though one was aware that what she was saying was worthy of being heard. Still, the relief when she said "amen" was palpable.

One left the service remembering the delight of the children's sermon—which, one assumes, is supposed to be delightful—

and the tedium of the adult sermon, which, one also assumes, is not supposed to be tedious. The difference between them was not that the adult sermon "said something," or said something "important," while the children's sermon did not. Both said important things. Nor was it because one was relatively short while the other was considerably longer. Those issues simply did not matter. It was also not because the pastor read her adult sermon badly. She did not. She read it carefully, putting as much animation into it as she could summon. What one went away from that service wishing, though, was that the adult sermon could have been as delightful and energizing, as spontaneous and zesty, as the children's sermon had been.

Why wasn't it? It was because the preacher, for whatever reasons, did not treat the delivery of the sermon with the same care and sophistication as she had the preparation of the sermon. If one were to ask this preacher if she could preach the same adult sermon without reading it from her manuscript, she most likely would say, no, she couldn't. "My public speaking just isn't that good," is the most common response to the question. Yet her children's sermon, despite its length, clearly indicated otherwise. She is an effective public speaker, whether her audience is young or old, whether she is standing or sitting. She is able to remember well what she wants to say, and she is clearly articulate and funny in saying whatever she has prepared. She *could* have delivered her adult sermon in the same way as the children's sermon. That's what all of us went away knowing that morning.

The same dramatic difference is often seen as well—though not in such dramatic juxtaposition—in sermons preached in so-called contemporary worship services and those preached in traditional services. The contemporary service is seen as a kind of youth service, or one for the young at heart, with its informality, praise music, guitars, and drums; the traditional service is for those who are older, those who prefer things more formal and liturgical, accompanied by organ music. Such preferences are natural and should not be resisted. Yet what has also emerged in many churches that have opted for the two-worship-service format is that each calls for its own kind of preaching. That is, one should preach informally in the contemporary service, which means just talking, without manuscript, while the traditional service calls for the sermon to be read from a manuscript. The difference invariably is the same as in my example of the children's sermon and the adult sermon at that metropolitan church: one is lively and captivating, usually not lightweight or ill prepared, while the other, though also well prepared, is often tedious and difficult to listen to.

What has happened is that countless preachers over the past two to three generations have been systematically taught that "real" preaching means reading their sermons verbatim from prepared manuscripts. Some even believe that the preacher must so attend to the words of his or her sermon that one *must* read from a manuscript in order for the sermon to work. What is lost in such thinking is the fact that, whatever else it is, the sermon is first and foremost an act of public speaking. There is not public speaking on one hand and preaching on the other. Preaching is public address before it is anything else, and if one expects one's sermon to be interesting, even compelling or captivating, then one's preaching must follow the basic rules of effective public speech. And the most fundamental rule of all effective public speaking—the ironclad rule of every Speech 101 class—is that one *cannot* read a manuscript to one's audience. Ironically, at a time when the sermons being prepared for delivery in both Protestant and Catholic churches everywhere are better than ever, many of those sermons are being lost by being read, word upon word, from the pulpit.

It is very important these days for all of us who preach to become the most effective public speakers that we can, following all of the basic rules of quality public address. This means learning to preach without manuscripts—and even, if we want to take our effectiveness to its highest point, to preach without notes. The argument of this book is that any preacher

11

can do this. This kind of preaching does not rest on one's speaking ability, but on one's understanding and practice of the disciplines of public address, along with a deep interest in what we wish to say. Moreover, all of this can be done, with a minimum of effort, on a regular weekly basis in any parish, large or small.

This book is designed to show the preacher how to do it, how to lay aside the manuscript and the sermon notes and go into the pulpit fully and thoroughly prepared to be the most effective public speaker—the most effective preacher— possible. It takes some courage, at least at first, but the payoff in the pulpit and in one's congregation will be nothing short of astounding, as one will discover the first Sunday one is willing to try it.

My own experience in preaching without notes goes back more than thirty-five years to another book, not unlike this one, that I read several times as a junior in a Christian college, as I looked forward to being a minister. It was written by Charles Koller, then president of Northern Baptist Theological Seminary in Chicago. It was called *Expository Preaching Without Notes,* and was published by Baker Book House. Between 1962 and 1979, it went through eleven printings, but it has long since been out of print. What follows in this book is not identical to that one. In fact, this book bears virtually no resemblance to that one, since so much about preaching, as well as our understandings about memory and public speaking, has changed dramatically since that one appeared.

I pay tribute to Koller, however, since this book sets out to do what his book did: to convince preachers that preaching without notes is urgently needed and that any preacher can do it and do it well. Koller urged that one preach without notes as a way of bringing the pulpit, which was in such sad shape in the early 1960s, back to life. That book made a believer out of me. As young as I was, I tried it and discovered that I could do it, that anyone could do it. What fun it was! What fun it has been! There was no looking back. Now, after years of my own preaching without notes, and after years of teaching public speaking and preaching in colleges, universities, and seminary, it is time for me to urge preachers to try it. What I say here is addressed particularly to those preachers who, with their manuscripts or notes, have become disillusioned or discouraged by what they experience when they preach week in and week out. It is also addressed to students preparing for ministry, students who are setting high ideals for themselves and who have lofty goals for what they want to accomplish in the pulpit.

This book begins with the "why": Why should one even consider preaching without manuscript or notes? It is a fair question, and one that needs to be addressed in some detail, which I will do in the introduction. Each of this book's four chapters discusses one of the four basic steps, or stages, to be followed in preparing and delivering a sermon to be preached without notes. Chapter one examines what goes into the preparation of a sermon that one preaches without notes. In a sense, this is a review, since any preacher who has taken a basic course in homiletics knows how to put a sermon together. Here, though, the question will be fairly specific: What special things need to be attended to in the preparation process when the sermon will be preached without notes? Chapter two, then, discusses the important process of outlining the sermon that one has prepared. Not surprisingly, the outline itself needs be specifically tailored for the task of preaching without notes. How that is done will be explained in some detail. Chapter three turns to the crucial issue of memorization. I will present what research has taught us about human memory, as well as specific directions on how to quickly, efficiently, and confidently memorize the outline and the supporting materials that one will need when the sermon is delivered. Chapter four, then, takes up the very crucial matter of how to finish the sermon by delivering it in the pulpit or on a platform. Here is where the preaching event is lifted to its highest level, although there are specific things to be done before that can happen.

Through each of these steps, I shall prepare a sample sermon, stage by stage, that I preached without notes. While the sermon is reproduced here as a manuscript, this is done only to allow the reader to see the movement toward the sermon's final preparation. No transcript is included here, since transcripts are, for the most part, unreadable. The "oral" art does not translate well, if at all, into the "written" art.

Like Koller's book, this one is small. But for the preacher who takes seriously what is said here, the experience in the pulpit will never be the same again. Nor, happily, will the sermon experience ever be the same again for those who gather week after week, eagerly anticipating that remarkable moment when the sermon begins.

Acknowledgments

I gratefully acknowledge the contributions made to this book by dozens of my preaching students at the Claremont School of Theology and at the Northwest House of Theological Studies in Oregon. I have pressed them hard, and they have invariably responded with graceful feedback and very good preaching. Would that I could name them all. A number of colleagues in homiletics have encouraged and assisted the book's publication, particularly Ron Allen of Christian Theological Seminary; Marjorie Suchocki, Kathy Black, and Woon Joo Baek of the Claremont School of Theology; and Eugene Lowry, now retired, of Saint Paul School of Theology. I thank them all. I am particularly indebted to Donald Treese, now retired from The United Methodist Church's General Board of Higher Education and Ministry. He took an early, and very strong, interest in my urgings about preaching without notes.

"O most gentle pulpiter! what tedious homily of love have you wearied your parishioners withal, and never cried 'Have patience, good people!' "

—William Shakespeare
As You Like It 3.2.163-66

Introduction

Why Preach Without Script or Notes?

Far and away the most extensive and insightful discussion of preaching without notes is found in one of the true classics of homiletical literature. It was written by John A. Broadus and first published in 1870 under the title, *A Treatise on the Preparation and Delivery of Sermons.*[1] In the last quarter of the book's 550 pages, Broadus discussed in detail the advantages and disadvantages of "three different ways of preparing and delivering sermons"—the reading of a manuscript, the drafted and fully memorized sermon, and the extemporaneous sermon, what he called "free speaking," by which he meant the sermon preached without manuscript, or preferably, for him, without notes.

Broadus first discussed the *reading* of a sermon manuscript, listing its advantages as greatly assisting the preacher's work of preparation "by rendering it easier to fix the mind upon the subject," as compelling the preacher toward "greater *completeness* of preparation," and as "[securing], in several respects, greater excellence of *style*." This is to say nothing of the method's advantage in placing the preacher more at ease, "both before and during the delivery." In having the sermon written out, Broadus said, the preacher "will be preserved, and knows that he [or she] will be, from any utter and mortifying failure."[2]

Nevertheless, for Broadus, reading something aloud, no matter how well or with how many asides, was not the same as public speaking. Reading was reading, a skill unto itself, and not public address. And if the sermon, in the end, was to rise to its highest level, it needed to be public address and not reading. He summed up his discussion of the read sermon like this:

> As to delivery itself, reading is of necessity less effective, and in most cases immensely less effective, for all the great purposes of oratory, than speaking. Greater coldness of manner is almost inevitable. If one attempts to be very animated or pathetic, it will look unnatural. The tones of voice are monotonous, or have a forced variety. The gestures are almost always unnatural, because it is not natural to gesticulate much in reading; and they scarcely ever raise us higher than to feel that really this man [or woman] reads almost like speaking.[3]

Broadus next discussed, briefly, the memorizing of scripted sermons—what he called the "recitation" of a sermon—which appears to have been fairly common in the latter part of the nineteenth century. The bottom line, for him then and for us now, is that it simply takes too much time to do this. Except for those who preach only occasionally, such memorization is not an option.

Broadus's most extensive discussion was reserved for extemporaneous preaching, or preaching without notes. His view was that if one could preach with notes, one could, and should, preach without notes. As he did with the other methods of preaching, he carefully mapped out the disadvantages of this free form of sermon delivery, noting that the major one is that it promotes a tendency to neglect careful preparation, to be sloppy or lazy in the making of the sermon. Another disadvantage is that this kind of speaking places the preacher in danger of "making blunders in statement," of saying things that are "irrelevant, ill-considered, improper, and sometimes, alas! even untrue."[4] Then there is the disadvantage that arises from the fact that "the success of an extemporaneous sermon is largely dependent upon the preacher's feelings at the time of delivery, and upon the circumstances." This means, he said, that the preacher is "liable to decided failure."[5]

The advantages of preaching extemporaneously, or without notes, though, are many, and Broadus carefully spelled them out. They came down to this summary statement, one parallel to what he said earlier about reading a manuscript:

> As to the delivery itself, it is only in extemporaneous speaking, of one or another variety, that [the sermon] can ever be perfectly natural, and achieve the highest effect. The ideal of speaking, it has been justly said, cannot be reached in any other way. Only thus will the voice, the action, the eye, be just what nature dictates, and attain their full power. And while painstaking culture vainly strives to read or recite precisely like speaking, the extemporaneous speaker may with comparative ease rise to the best delivery of which he [or she] is capable.[6]

There is one other advantage of extemporaneous speaking, which Broadus discussed in some detail. It is, as he put it, that "with the masses of the people, it is the *popular* method." As a preacher, he said, one should never play to the masses as far as one's message is concerned. But in the method of delivering the sermon—which he called "a mere question of [expedience]"—the popular preference "is an exceedingly important consideration." There are, Broadus acknowledged, "fastidious people who greatly prefer reading or recitation" from the pulpit; but they are seldom more than a small minority. There are even, he says, some congregations that "have been educated into a toleration of reading, but it is almost always an unwilling acquiescence."[7]

Broadus wrote toward the end of a notable century of oratory, in the years before mass media and the emergence of communication research that accompanied the rise of radio and eventually television. What is remarkable, in retrospect, is that everything Broadus said about public, collective speech—and preaching—became even more thoroughly understood and underscored in the twentieth century. What came to be called speech communication brought with it a proliferation of research in both universities and corporations. In particular, we now know much more about the complex nature of public speech, public address, than Broadus did, but what we know only enhances the arguments that he articulated with such care more than a century ago.

Before we expand on the question of *why* one should consider preaching without notes, it is important to clarify our use of the terms that surround this process, particularly one that we have already encountered in Broadus. To do this, we pose the question of what it means to preach without notes, something that should not go unasked. It means that the preacher preaches without the prompting of any kind of written material during the sermon's delivery, regardless of whether standing in or behind a pulpit or on an open platform, stage, or dias.

Preaching without notes is much more complicated than that, however. Two terms are most often associated with speaking, or preaching, without manuscript or notes. The first is to call it "extemporaneous" speaking, or preaching, the term that Broadus used. But if one takes the word apart etymologically, it means "out of time," or speaking without benefit of time. Most often, at least today, this suggests one speaking without benefit of preparation time, or without preparation. That, though, was not what Broadus meant by it; if that is what it conjures up for the reader here, then preaching without manuscript or notes is not extemporaneous at all. Sadly, whenever one hears bad preaching without notes—that is, when the note-free preacher rambles, goes off on tangents, hems and haws, or has difficulty ending the sermon—it is invariably because that preacher has not prepared, or has not prepared well enough.

The second term often associated with this is improvised speaking, or improvisational preaching. This word refers to not having made advance provision for something, in this case, public speaking. It means to speak even though one has not prepared in advance something specific to say. We are familiar with improvisational theater in which actors take the stage not knowing what they will perform. Usually, it is left to the audience to suggest the scenes or sketches that the performers act out. From this perspective, preaching without script or notes is not improvisational. Preaching without script or notes is never done "off the cuff," or "on the spur of the moment," even though every preacher knows the experience of being unexpectedly called on to "say a few words." This, however, is not what we have in mind for preaching without notes.

What we are emphasizing is that the sermon preached without script or notes is a well-developed, meticulously crafted sermon, open to the guidance of the Holy Spirit, but prepared under the same constraints of procedure, time, and energy that guide every preacher week in and week out. As I shall discuss in this book, however, preparing a sermon to be preached without notes is different in important respects from preparing one to be delivered from manuscript or extensive notes; those differences provide the focus of the chapters that follow. Primarily, to preach without notes is to make adjustments in one's sermon preparation process and time, but this can readily be done by anyone who knows the fundamentals of sermon making. The point is that the time required for preparing a sermon to be preached without notes is no more or less than is required to make any sermon ready for the pulpit.

There is no question that preaching without notes has been given a bad name by some preachers who have regularly resorted to extemporaneous or improvised talks, sermons with precious little preparation and even less substance. For the most part, these are preachers who have come to place little importance on preaching. Church people, they believe, do not care much for preaching; so why should the preacher give it very much attention? These are preachers who rank preaching very low on their list of ministerial or pastoral duties, and, as a result, the small amount of time they give it is commensurate, they think, with what it deserves.

Such a view of preaching, however, does not square at all with recent studies of active churchgoers, including younger Christians. One of the most detailed of these studies was carried out by the Association of United Methodist Theological Schools. It was based on interviews with more than seven hundred United Methodist laity and clergy at thirteen regional events across the country beginning in 1994. The final national report, based on some four hundred hours of conversation with these people, was issued under the title, *Agenda 21: United Methodist Ministry for a New Century.* While discussing numerous pastoral skills needed within congregational life, the report concluded that

> there is strong consensus that . . . preaching is the most important skill in ordained ministry. The church desperately wants preaching that effectively relates the gospel to human experience. . . . The need for improvement in this skill has been apparent for so long that laity are distressed as to why seminary and church leadership "don't get it."

The report added:

> There is widespread disappointment that so much preaching lacks enthusiasm for the gospel . . . , for the church in which it is proclaimed, and for the congregation. . . . Laity yearn for good preaching, and both church and seminary need to account for deficiencies in this important skill. . . .
>
> Through preaching . . . the congregation gains confidence in a pastor's leadership in other areas; it is, simply put, the most powerful visibility the pastor has. . . . Too little emphasis on preaching by seminaries sets students up for serious difficulties in the future. The schools should seriously listen to local churches on this matter and undertake the necessary reforms to better train their students in the art and skill of preaching, including its public speaking aspects.[8]

Two things in particular arise from this statement, however; one overtly, the other somewhat covertly. The first is that preachers who play down the importance of preaching are out of sync with what their congregations want most, which is the highest quality preaching possible. The second thing in the statement, however, appears in the last sentence. It is that laypeople tend to believe that preachers, by and large, are not doing the best possible job that they could do in the pulpit, and that their chief failing is not theological or pastoral; it is a failure in public speaking. Hence, reforms or changes are necessary in order for preachers to rise to those highest levels desired by congregations. And the highest form of public address, as Broadus and so many other preaching scholars have since emphasized, is that which is done in a well-prepared, highly disciplined fashion—but without notes.[9]

What makes the well-prepared, well-delivered sermon preached without notes such an exhilarating and frequently memorable experience? There are three basic answers to this question, answers that arise from years of research in speech communication and rhetoric. We will examine each of them briefly, fully aware that numerous preachers have preached faithfully and well for years with their manuscripts and notes, yet suggesting, too, that those same preachers would do well to reexamine whether they might raise their preaching to an even higher level of effectiveness now and for the future.

To Maximize Connectedness

The first reason for preaching without notes is because it makes possible the fullest and most intense bonding between the preacher and those who share the preaching. This is not to say that good manuscript or note preachers do not connect to some degree with those who hear their sermons. Often they do. It is a matter of degree, however. If one wishes to create and sustain the *strongest* bond possible between a given speaker and audience (congregants), that can only be accomplished when one preaches without notes. While other factors can influence this bonding—such as the charisma of the speaker, the nature of the shared occasion, the technical skill of the preacher—all other things being equal, the preacher without notes establishes a stronger bond by way of the sermon with his or her congregants than one who uses script or notes.

This reflects the classic power of public speech from its ancient to its most modern forms. Thinking out words carefully and speaking them with naturalness and energy, without visible prompting, can create mental, emotional, even spiritual connections with an audience that no other form of public address can match. It is not easy to describe, let alone explain, this bonding power, and yet anyone who has ever been held spellbound listening to someone speak—as we all have been at some time or other—knows the indescribable magic of that experience. Even if one is sitting with hundreds of other people, a speaker can literally sustain a rapt hush over the entire crowd, with every person absorbed in the communal experience. Everyone becomes riveted to the speaker, shutting out virtually everything around. In such a situation, time stops. No one looks at watches or clocks. When it is over, even though significant time has passed, it seems like it has only been a few moments. One was caught up in the experience, lost in it, not wanting it to stop.

There is more to it than this, though. Without notes, human passion is set free, and passion is as close to the cement of human bonding as we ever get. This is not to say that those who read manuscripts from the pulpit never experience or communicate any passion. Again, they often do. But even then, it is virtually inevitable (as Broadus put it) that the passion is muted, since passion is not a normal by-product of reading. In preaching without notes, though, the passions of the preacher become—or *can* become—fully engaged. As the preacher's passions become engaged, the congregation's passions are also engaged, often to match the level of the preacher's. One sees this most profoundly in the often overt preacher/congregation interactions of African American churches. This expression of passion by preacher and congregation can take a thousand different forms, and it is seldom, if ever, expressed in exactly the same way in any two preaching situations. But in whatever form it appears—when it is genuine, unimpeded by script or notes—it is often electrifying to those who experience it.

Some homileticians and preachers believe that the true power of public address lies not in passion but in words, in poetic, picturesque language. This, in fact, is often given as a reason why one must carefully write out and then read the written sermon to one's congregants. Every word in it must be carefully chosen, evoking just the right images and sensations, and then those words, once chosen, must be carefully read aloud from the pulpit so that the evocations of the language can be experienced again among those who share the words.

There is no denying the importance of words, their evocative power, their poetic creation of imagery. Speaking well includes knowing how to choose one's language; it includes knowing the sensuality of words and phrases, and being able to create original and provocative pictures with one's speech. That is still the surface of effective public address, however. Research has taught us that the most effective public speech is only secondarily about words, about language. Invariably, what people listen to and for in public address are not the words themselves, not even the images conjured up by the words as they are spoken. What they watch for and are most sensitive to are the feelings, the emotions, out of which the words that are spoken arise. They listen for what is behind and under the words.

When a speaker demonstrates that he or she feels deeply, even intensely, about the subject being talked about, and gives voice to those passionate ideas and feelings, then the words invariably will be the right words, whether they are poetic or not. They will be spoken not because they are the right words or because they are particularly vivid or poetic, but because they are the only words capable of expressing, at that moment, the deepest stirrings of the speaker. Because of that, those nonpoetic, unplanned words will often become poetic in the speaking.

It may seem that in placing the emphasis on the preacher's underlying passion rather than on the words of the sermon the result will be an anti-intellectual experience—satisfying only at some emotional level. Exactly the opposite, however, is the case. Even though some sermons preached without notes certainly can be all emotion and no intellectual substance—something quite unacceptable—that is not the case with good preaching sans manuscript and notes. On the contrary; good preaching without manuscript or notes can be one of the richest intellectual activities that one can experience. Even though everything is well prepared, the preacher stands in front of people literally thinking out loud. The ideas have been worked through, both consciously and unconsciously; but even after the ideas have been outlined and memorized, they are refined and rethought right up to and even through the course of the sermon's delivery. Moreover, as preachers without notes have known for a long time, when one has prepared well, some of the best and more inspiring ideas that one ends up articulating can come to the preacher's mind only in the heat of the speaking itself. It is not that the sermon preached without notes is either intellect or emotion. Instead, it can be, and often is, the sermon that best blends the two dimensions together. And, in the end, it is that remarkable blend that achieves the highest level of bonding between preacher and a roomful of congregants.

To Maximize Participation

The second reason for preaching without notes is because such a sermon, by its inductive, emergent nature, invites the participation of congregants more than any other kind of sermon delivery can. We may explain it like this: It is commonplace in homiletics these days to talk about the rise of the so-called inductive sermon. Most preachers by now have learned to enjoy preaching inductive sermons. In the inductive form, one tries to create tension, even suspense, by not letting congregants know what is going to happen next as the sermon unfolds. It is like telling a story that the teller knows while keeping the hearers guessing what is around the next corner. So this kind of sermon (or story) invites, and often even requires, those who share it to become involved in it; what the hearer invariably does is "run ahead" of the teller, and, as everyone who has listened to stories knows, it is fun to do.

A preacher can, of course, either write out and read an inductive sermon or prepare detailed inductive notes for use in the pulpit. But something else is very important here. Good speech communicators tell us that *how* one speaks can also be either of a deductive or an inductive nature. What contributes to the most effective public speaking is the inductively delivered speech, or, in our case, sermon. The difference is that in the deductive speech mode the audience perceives that almost every word is pre-planned. In the inductive speech mode, the audience senses, or knows, that the words are *not* planned in advance; neither the speaker nor the audience knows what the next words, or the next sentence, will be. Everything ahead stays up in the air; everything is unfolding. The words being spoken are actually emerging as the speech (or sermon) itself is progressing. This is inductive delivery, and, like the inductive sermon form, it too is shot through with tension and even suspense about what the speaker is going to say next.

Moreover, induction, as we know with sermon form, is highly participatory, more so than the older deductive forms of the sermon. When an inductive delivery, such as preaching without notes, is wedded to the inductive form of a sermon's construction, one creates the most participatory sermon that it is possible to create.

To Reflect Authentic Witness

A third reason for preaching without notes is because, in a world in which cynicism about what to believe or not believe is everywhere, the pulpit can become one of those rare places where lively witnessing and testifying take place. I state the matter like that, knowing full well that many preachers for years have read their manuscripts and, in doing so, have given voice to their Christian witness. But something deeper must be grasped here: In order for one's Christian witness to be as moving as it can possibly be, that witness must appear to those who receive it to come "from the preacher's heart" and "not from a page of the preacher's sermon." One can move people by reading or speaking from notes, but one cannot move them very far. If that sounds harsh, I do not mean for it to. To give one's most powerful witness, at least for the majority of people, it is necessary to stop reading, stop following one's notes, set the paper aside, and just stand up and talk. Tell us what is going on with you, what you have learned, and what you now experience. Tell us from your heart, and we will know that what you say is true—if not true for all of us, at least true for you. And that, in itself, will mean a great deal.

Policitians and business officials often watch what they say very carefully, so every word of every speech must be scripted and read—no slips of the tongue are allowed. But enormous pains are taken and technological advances utilized to create a full-scale illusion of nonscripted speaking, of speaking spontaneously, "from the heart." The technology that places a TelePrompTer displaying the words to be spoken directly in front of the camera's lens is now stock-in-trade for the most formal public speaking. Underlying it all, however, is the clear understanding that somehow one will only appear truly believable if one gets rid of the script and the notes and just talks. Most preachers have no access to such technology, but the meaning is clear: "Just speaking" without script or notes may not ensure credibility among one's congregants—other things may still interfere with that—but the first step toward raising the power of one's most credible witness in the pulpit is to set aside the manuscript and the notes.

Some Personal Responses

It is not enough at this point, though, merely to review some of the reasons why the preacher should preach without manuscript or notes. It is often the case that a preacher may acknowledge that preaching without notes does, theoretically, result in better sermons. That preacher is left saying something like: "I wish I could preach without notes too, but I cannot. I wish I could, but . . . "; or, "I would if I could, but. . . ." When the preacher finishes these sentences with "but," it usually means one of two things.

The first is the feeling of intimidation. For many preachers, the very idea of delivering a sermon without manuscript or notes sounds impossible. They say "I know that there are a few preachers who can do that, but most of us cannot; at least I am not one of those who can" or "No, I have never tried it, but I am quite sure that I could not do it. In fact, I know I could not do it." The statement is made as often by a seasoned, working preacher as it is by a beginning seminarian.

Most often, the intimidation pressure focuses on one's memory. One might think "I know that preaching without notes means that one relies on one's memory. Mine has never been very good, and it seems to give me more problems the older I get." Or "I just get terribly nervous and every time I get nervous I forget things. I never have to worry about it when my manuscript is in front of me. I wish I could do otherwise, but I'm afraid I just do not have what it takes."

What we know, however, is that the human memory is a remarkably underutilized capability. One learns to memorize and then practices doing it. Just like any other skill that one sharpens, the more one practices using the memory, the better one gets at it. The fact is that one's memory is not a problem as far as preaching without notes is concerned; one's *confidence* in one's memory is invariably the problem. It is a matter of commitment, discipline, and trust in oneself—and, yes, in God.

31

The second objection often heard is more theological and less personal. While it takes various forms, its general assertion is that some sermons, and indeed some parts of almost all sermons, simply do not lend themselves to being preached without notes. Some sermons, in fact, virtually require a manuscript. The argument is that when one deals with matters of theology or doctrine, considerable care and precision is required, the kind of precision that calls for every word or phrase to be carefully scripted. One does not want to be too glib, that is, when dealing with holy tradition or with biblical complexities or even with matters of practical piety. It is too easy in our day to be misunderstood, and the way to prevent that misunderstanding, it is suggested, is to write out the sermon in manuscript or at least as a highly detailed outline.

Such statements, though, need to be rethought. Preachers today are well educated, most of them from good seminaries where they learned well the lessons of their own faith traditions as well as of the larger theological perspectives. Preachers, moreover, have usually passed ordination examinations in which they are asked to articulate complex theological issues and problems without any outside help, without crib notes. They are asked to talk about theological matters in ways that would make sense to laypeople. Preachers, by and large, know how to do this. Preachers study and put things in their own words. They know how to articulate, often in highly original ways, matters of both theology and doctrine.

Congregants, too, are smart people. They appreciate and learn from straightforward explanations of things, even theological things. They do not worry about the preacher tripping over a word or a phrase; they understand how we all talk. They also want to learn theology and doctrine. So the word comes unspoken to the preacher from the congregants: "Tell us about your faith, and ours. Tell us about theology, what it is and how it works. Tell us what you have learned about it and how you have come to think about it and internalize it yourself. Share with us the issues of theology and how that theology impinges on us. Share stories with us. Give us reason to laugh. But talk to us about the hard stuff as well. Don't read it to us. Talk to us. Struggle through it with us. Tell us what is behind the language of the creed that we just said together, but do so without jargon and the big words of the books, and even without worrying about how you wrote it down while you were in your study. Just talk to us." Congregants want that.

But we should pause here. We have thought about the "why" of preaching without notes; it is time to turn to the "how" of it. How can one do this? How does one go about trying it out? Those are the questions to which we turn in this book. It should be said at the outset, though, that what follows here is a working model, at best; a schematic. It remains for every preacher to adapt the model to her or his own unique inclinations and circumstances. What is important is that one try it, that one compare its result with how one now delivers the sermon. There is good reason to believe that this approach to pulpit work best carries out Augustine's dictum about the gospel: *Veritas pateat, veritas placeat, veritas moveat,* "Make the truth plain, make it pleasing, make it moving."

33

Chapter One

Planning the Sermon Without Notes: Monday and Tuesday

The decision to preach a sermon without notes should be made *before* the sermon is prepared, not after. This is because preaching without notes requires one to prepare in some strikingly different ways than if one plans to write out and preach from a manuscript, or even to preach from an extensively worked outline. It is not, in other words, just a matter of "having a sermon" and deciding to preach it without notes. That can be done, of course, but usually with considerable difficulty, and the result is often not very satisfying either to preacher or to congregants.

This does not mean, though, that there is only one way to prepare the sermon for preaching without notes. Just as there are many different styles and types of sermons, so preachers learn to prepare and preach sermons in many different ways. Students in seminary homiletics classes hear different things from different professors, as they undoubtedly should, and the continuing appearance of new books on how to preach in today's world provides a strong sense that there is no one way to carry out this most important of pastoral responsibilities. Despite such differences, however, the preacher still has to decide, at some point, what to say in the sermon and then how to get it said. For our purposes here, the question is whether the preacher goes about the planning and preparation of the sermon any differently after deciding to preach it without notes.

The answer is *yes*. It is not that one must learn new ways of preparing a sermon. What this decision means is that the preacher will emphasize and even concentrate on certain aspects of the sermon preparation process knowing that he or she will enter the pulpit or step onto the platform without notes. It will also mean that sermon preparation time will be used in different ways when one plans to preach without notes. Finally, it will mean that what we might call the "emotional" disciplines of sermon preparation will be different, since what happens in the hours leading up to the sermon's delivery will be altered significantly in order to preach without notes. Knowing all this in advance makes the task of preparing and preaching the sermon without notes much easier and much less time-consuming; it also ensures that the sermon preached will be far more effective than it would otherwise be.

So we will begin with the sermon-planning process itself, starting with what amounts to a brief review of the major elements in shaping the sermon's content. We do so, however, not for the sake of review, but in order to explain what makes the sermon without notes different in the planning. In addition, here and in the remaining chapters of this book, we will tie the steps in the overall process to specific days of the sermon-making week. We do this because one learns very quickly that preaching well without notes must be a highly disciplined process requiring nothing less than a conscious commitment on the part of the preacher. One can, of course, try one or two sermons without notes to see how it works, or if one likes it. But one will never become truly effective at preaching without notes unless one is willing to do it week in and week out, growing better and better at it over time. It is a learned skill, based on practiced activities, and the daily and weekly procedures of planning and preparation are indispensable to its success. The payoffs, though, are beyond anything that one who has not tried it can imagine. The following basic plan should be carried out over the first two days of one's workweek for the following Sunday.

Different preachers begin the sermon from different points, just as any given preacher can begin different sermons from different starting points as well. Sometimes one begins with a text, as those who are lectionary preachers virtually always do. Other preachers begin with an idea, a topic, something that he or she particularly wants to say in a given circumstance or on a particular occasion. One can, of course, go back and forth— sometimes a text kicks off planning, sometimes a topic that one takes to a particular text generates the idea. Despite their interchangeability, both of these starting points are very important, and with whichever idea one begins—text or topic—the other must be taken up next, usually in interaction with the first. So we will consider each of them briefly here, beginning with the biblical text, whether it is assigned or chosen by the preacher.

Working With the Text

Frequently, the preacher turns to a biblical text without any particular idea about what the sermon will be about, let alone actually say. When this happens, one usually depends on the text to provide at least the kernel of content from which the final sermon will grow. As every preacher knows, though, this encounter with a biblical text—*any* biblical text—is one of the most complex dimensions of the entire sermon-making process. For some preachers, the words of the Bible are the very words of God, and sermon planning amounts to finding ways to repeat those words in new ways without altering what is taken to be their once-and-for-all meaning. For other preachers, Jesus is the Word to be found in the midst of the Bible's words, so one peels away the layers of language in order to discover and preach the real historical Jesus who came to earth as the Son of God. For still other preachers, the Bible is a complex collection of assorted historical documents that arose from the varied communities that developed into churches from the late first century through the second and third centuries; so what we have in the Bible is the record of several distinct faith traditions, all built around a figure who was thought to be God come to earth. Moreover, it is these various historical traditions that have coalesced into the multiple religious groupings called churches or denominations in which we who preach have chosen to take up our lives.

I sketch this to indicate the extraordinary, though often overlooked, range of attitudes that working preachers today bring to the Bible. It is one's view of the Bible, moreover, that dictates how one interacts with a biblical text for preaching. One can read a text in order to listen to it and speak what it says, or one can carry out a kind of dialogue with a text, hearing it but talking back to it, being suspicious of it, or even rejecting its assertions or implications. Despite all of this, the sermon, in my view, should somehow take account of the text. The biblical text, that is, should be part of the sermon; but more than that, the sermon should reflect the preacher's own overt dealings with the text, whatever form they take. We live in a time when laypeople of all kinds want desperately to know about the Bible—what it is, where it came from, why and how it has come to be understood as "Word (capital W), or word (lowercase w), of God." Candor about the Bible and its texts seems to be a particularly pressing obligation facing the preacher today—whatever the preacher's tradition or theological orientation.[1]

So the preacher may begin sermon planning by working in a text. One uses all of the exegetical tools, presuppositions, and procedures that one has been taught within a theological tradition. Whatever the processes, however, if one is planning a sermon to be preached without notes, one thing becomes paramount: You take detailed notes on your examination of the text. You can say, "Of course I take notes when I do my exegetical work," but the point is that when you work on or think through a text that will be part of a sermon preached without notes, it is even more important that your findings and thoughts be very carefully and meticulously recorded. This, in fact, is the first key difference in how one prepares to preach without manuscript or notes.

If the text is a story or a narrative, whether from the Hebrew Bible or the New Testament, even the details of the story need to be written down. This is because if a preacher chooses to use the story in the sermon, as is often the case, he or she must actually learn the story in its color and detail in order to bring it to life. If a preacher chooses to retell the Bible story, it must be told well, and from memory. The first step in doing that is writing down the story's progression and details, including the names, actions, and interactions of its characters. One can reply, "If I decide to use the text's story in the sermon, *then* I will write down and learn the story's detail." Keep in mind, however, that often the decision of whether or not to use the story in the sermon arises from a more intimate sense of the story's own inner workings. In other words, a pastor often decides to use the biblical story as part of the sermon *because* it has been written out.

The same is true of virtually every other kind of biblical material with which one chooses to preach, whether a psalm from the Hebrew Bible, a section from one of the Minor Prophets, a part of a Pauline letter, or even a pericope from the Apocalypse of John.

You should also record as fully as possible what you learn exegetically about a text, regardless of how the information is gathered. Your notes should include your own thoughts and interactions with the text. In the course of sermon planning and preparation, it is easy to forget important ideas that cross one's mind in even the most casual of ruminations. Notes must be taken so that the ideas, however fleeting, are not lost. Often they are not easy to call back. When such ideas, along with notes about historical backgrounds, textual or literary insights and so forth, are written down as one goes, they become initially etched, however faintly, in one's mind. This is the first important step toward preaching the resulting sermon without notes. There is much more to do, to be sure, but this is where it most efficiently begins.

With this in mind, let me begin the illustration that will

track through this entire book: the preparation of one sermon from beginning to end. This sermon was, for me, one of a series on little-known characters of the Bible, characters whose influence far outweighed their actual presence in biblical narratives. The character for this sermon is John Mark. Like almost everyone reared in the church, I knew a little about John Mark. I knew about the breakup between Paul and Barnabas over Mark; about the fact that John Mark was widely believed to be the author of the first Gospel to be written, at least our first canonical Gospel; and I accepted, over time in seminary and study, the view held by a growing number of scholars that Mark had written his Gospel not early but late— in the weeks or months after the destruction of Jerusalem and the Temple by the Romans in A.D. 70. I also had come to the view that Mark's Gospel provides the paradigm, in a sense, on which the other canonical Gospels were formed.

Beyond that, I was going to have to do some hunting. As it was, I knew I would not be working with a single text, but with several, and that the story of Mark that I would end up telling would, in fact, be constructed out of several texts scattered throughout the New Testament. I looked up John Mark in a Bible dictionary. I was surprised at how few references there are to him. I knew that in my sermon I was going to have to know these, so I took careful notes on each one.

The first reference to John Mark is in Acts 12:12. Herod, in trying to please the Jews, began to arrest and even murder some Christian leaders. James, the brother of John, was put to death with the sword, the text says. Peter, too, was arrested and held for what was to have been a public trial after Passover. The church, though, was praying, and Peter was rescued from the prison at night by an angel. He made his way, we are told, to the house of Mary, "the mother of John whose other name was Mark." The suggestion is that John Mark was still a boy, perhaps a teenage boy, at the time, but it is clear from the text's account that John Mark knew Peter. Strikingly, the last reference to John Mark in the New Testament comes at the end of 1 Peter 5:13

where the text says, "Your sister church in Babylon, chosen together with you, sends you greetings; and so does my son Mark." Since these quotations are fairly brief, I write them down on one of my note cards.

The next reference to Mark is in Acts 12:25. Barnabas had brought Saul, the new and feared convert, to Jerusalem for the first time—no doubt a fearful event for all involved. But Barnabas was vouching for Saul, now a Christian. When their visit to Jerusalem was finished, Barnabas and Saul returned to Antioch, from which they had come, taking with them, we are told, "John, whose other name was Mark." Once back in Antioch, Barnabas and Saul are set aside for missions work and quickly (it seems) sent on their way. They went down to Seleucia and sailed from there to Cyprus; and, again a simple note, "And they had John also to assist them" (Acts 13:5).

Then, a few verses later, comes that single line—one that should sound ominous, but does not. Verse 13 says that "Paul and his companions set sail from Paphos and came to Perga in Pamphylia. John, however, left them and returned to Jerusalem." Everything else proceeds in what appears to be a well-planned fashion. The trip ends in 14:26 and 27, with Paul and Barnabas reporting back to the church in Antioch "all that God had done with them." Chapter 14 ends, then, with the note that "they stayed there with the disciples for some time." How much time we do not know.

Chapter 15 tells the story of the ordeal of the Jerusalem council in which Paul and Barnabas were deeply involved; but then, at the end of the chapter they are back home in Antioch when Paul suggests to Barnabas that it would be good for them to revisit the churches that they started on their first trip. More than likely, two to three years had gone by since that trip was completed. It is at that point that we have the most intense light thrown on John Mark, clearly the best known dimension of his story. Barnabas suggests that John Mark would like to go on their planned trip and Paul reacts with an intensity that can only be inferred by the text. "Over my dead body" would be a rough but not inaccurate translation of the Greek text. It is not difficult to sense the profound emotion on both sides, emotion that results in this breakup of two very close friends and companions. Barnabas insists that John Mark will go, and Paul insists that he will not. Barnabas makes clear that if John Mark is not allowed to go, then he will not go either. Paul, surprisingly, accepts that. They part company. Paul chooses Silas as his new partner and the text says that Barnabas and Mark sailed for Cyprus, where, more than likely, both of them—cousins we later learn—were from. The story of Acts follows Paul and Silas. From that point on for many years we know nothing of Mark.

What I am writing here are the notes that I took as I tracked through the few texts concerning Mark. I am trying to put the text's story, with quotations at appropriate points, into my own words. I want to be able to tell these pieces as a story, even though I am not quite sure yet how the story will end. However, the Bible dictionary has given me three other references for John Mark. The first is in Paul's Colossian letter. I am already starting to create what, for me, will be a time line of Mark's life. The second missionary tour, the one that went on with Silas instead of Barnabas and Mark, can probably be dated as beginning in about 49 or 50, but the Colossian letter is quite late in Paul's life. It may have been written during his first Roman imprisonment, that period of more than two years when he was "in chains" but held in a house of some kind. Most scholars put that as being from 60 to 62 or even 63, not long before his martyrdom. So at least ten years will have passed between the blowup over Mark and the Colossian letter. At the end of that letter is a completely unexpected note: "Aristarchus my fellow prisoner greets you, as does Mark the cousin of Barnabas" (Col. 4:10). It is then followed by the telltale line: "You have received instructions—if he [Mark] comes to you, welcome him." What instructions? Mark has a reputation that the churches know very well. Is he considered untrustworthy? A deserter when the going gets rough? What?

Where and how did they hear such things? Who wrote instructions to whom? And what might this person have said? I do not know—*we* do not know—but my notes have me trying to spell out my thoughts as I go.

More important: What took place in the time between the breakup of Paul and Barnabas some ten years earlier and this point when John Mark is obviously back with Paul? Did Mark ask Paul's forgiveness? And Paul then took him back? Since we have no idea as to what actually happened, we are somewhat free to use our imaginations. My suggestion is that their separation lasted a long time, and that whatever healing took place did so not long before the Colossian letter was written. But Mark came back, and Paul accepted that. And now Paul writes a note of commendation on his behalf to a church that clearly does not think well of him. We must piece it together as best we can.

There are two other references to John Mark, one probably written by Paul at the same time the Colossian letter was written. This reference is in the short note to Philemon—a man most believe Paul never met—on behalf of Onesimus, the slave who had run away from Philemon. At the end of that note, Paul writes, "Epaphras, my fellow prisoner in Christ Jesus, sends greetings to you, and so do Mark" along with a few others (vv. 23-24). Then, in 2 Timothy 4:11, in a text whose authorship must remain a mystery to us, but which is probably written on behalf of Paul, or perhaps from words that the writer heard Paul speak at some point in the past, this note: "Get Mark and bring him with you, for he is useful in my ministry." That is all, but there is urgency in the line. There is no way for us to know when this was written either, even though it is placed by its author in Paul's lifetime. Nonetheless, we know that Paul and Mark have become close by the end of Paul's life in about 65, and we also know that in another five or six years someone—and for many of us it is John Mark— will step up and write the Gospel story that will forever change the world.

There is one other thing. Some scholars, though certainly

not all, believe that the aside found in Mark 14:51 is Mark calling himself the "young man" who fled naked into the night when Jesus was seized in the garden. But we do not know. With these texts, though, I plan to construct a story, a biography made of bits and pieces of text. Since I am going to preach my sermon on John Mark without notes, I know even at this stage that I am going to tell this story, drawing explicitly on these texts. So I have taken careful notes. I know already that I must learn them. I will want to tell them, very much as I am already starting to do here.

How one goes about this very careful study and notation of biblical text will vary from sermon to sermon, story to story, text to text. I take some time with the Mark texts to indicate what they called for in my preparation. If one works with a single text, working through it line for line, one will do the same thing—thinking through both what is on the surface and what might lie beneath the surface. No two sets of material, in my experience, are ever quite alike; nor can one say in advance just how one will go about learning the text. There is no question, though, that I am able to see ahead enough at this point to know that my memory work has already begun. Although I don't do this deliberately, this is the place where I begin learning the various pieces of my text's story. This is as it should be. Suffice it to say that if you wait until the sermon is complete to begin learning the text for preaching without notes, you are making the overall sermon preparation much more complicated than it needs to be.

From Topic to Bottom Line

Earlier, we noted that sometimes the preacher begins sermon work with the text, having little idea as to what the sermon will be about. That was the way that my sermon on John Mark began. Actually, in that case I started with a character, knowing a bit about the details of the story, but learning much more as I pieced together the various texts and references as I found them. Still, though, I did not know what the sermon would be about. I did not know, that is, what topic the story of John Mark would actually raise to which I could give voice in the sermon. More than that, I did not know when I began the exegetical note taking what I would end up wanting to say in the sermon, let alone have any idea how to say it. Deciding these two things, however—what the sermon would be about and what I would say about that topic—would be done, at least initially, from my reflections on the textual materials. Before I add that movement to my John Mark sermon preparation, however, the issue of what the sermon will say needs careful consideration, particularly since the sermon under preparation will be preached without notes.

While any sermon that one preaches requires focus and clarity, that requirement is amplified many times over when the sermon will be preached without notes. Clarity begins with being able to say, specifically, what the sermon is about. The topic can, of course, be anything that the preacher deems to be of theological, ethical, or spiritual significance. But the sermon cannot be about more than one topic. Even multiple topics that one believes need to be examined in relation to one another present enormous problems. Focus becomes difficult. Memorizing becomes problematic and a clean movement through the sermon is not easy to pull off. One is virtually forced to select one topic and then let other issues, even related ones, be subordinate to the dominant topic. Moreover, virtually every text with which one works easily lends itself to a wide variety of topics. This is why any text can be preached multiple times, since each potential topic can open the door to a different sermon, often a radically different one.

In working through my notes on John Mark, two topics become clear to me. One is forgiveness, which calls for a focus not so much on Mark—though that would be possible—as on Paul. Paul's psyche through the entire long period of his relation to John Mark is worth a close examination. But I want the focus this time to be on John Mark, the extended course of his life as I can reconstruct it from these texts. So the topic that forms in my mind, generally speaking, has to do with how a life undergoes change. I can now say that I know what the sermon will be about.

From there, though, the sermon gets more specific fairly quickly, since I can now sketch the overview of Mark's life: from what appears to be his boyhood, through his early experiences with his cousin Barnabas, and with Paul, to his later years—also with Paul—including his interaction with the larger church. I am ready to move from the topic to a more clearly defined sense of what my sermon will actually say. It will be the bottom line of the sermon, and it will be designed to provide a sharpness of focus and clarity from which I can plan, prepare, and finally hold the overall sermon sharply in view as I preach it.

Homiletically, there is some debate about the need for a bottom-line statement, a single sentence, as it were, that sums up everything in the sermon. When one is talking about preaching without notes, however, there is no debate. Parenthetically, it is my view that the habit of writing out and reading full sermon manuscripts in the pulpit—manuscripts that are essentially essays, however fluid their style—is largely responsible for our having lost sight of the importance of having a single, well-defined statement around which the entire sermon is constructed. Essays are, by their nature, complicated statements; sermons preached without notes, by their nature, cannot be complicated statements. Essays are meant to be read in private as words on a page; sermons are meant to be heard as spoken events. In teaching speech of any kind, one emphasizes the need for a single major idea per speaking event; and everything in that event must be shaped by, built around, and ultimately contribute to that one major idea. It is a fact of how human public address works, whatever kind it is. When one decides to make that public address without script or notes, the need for that single controlling idea is not only important, it is essential.

Beyond that, the shift in recent years from deductive to

inductive sermon construction has not removed the need for one central idea as a basis for the sermon. What it has done is shift where and how that idea is presented in the sermon. In deductive preaching forms, that idea is stated up front, as what used to be called the sermon's proposition; everything that follows as the sermon progresses argues for that propositional statement or assertion. In inductive preaching, that one central statement is still there, but, as Fred Craddock used to explain to his preaching classes, the statement is moved from the top to the *bottom* of the blank page that will fill up as the sermon. The statement will emerge from the sermon's discussion, finally reaching actual verbalization only at or near the sermon's end.

The sermon to be preached without notes will be—or, in my judgment, *should* be—an inductive sermon. So the sermon's central statement, its benchmark for focus, clarity, and simplicity, is essential. In the case of my sermon on John Mark, the statement was much easier to draw than I expected it to be. The sermon is about John Mark's life, particularly from his early experience with the apostle Paul to his later experiences, culminating in his writing of his Gospel, what I take to be our First Gospel. I will frame the statement for my sermon around the early life failure (is that the best word?) of John Mark, the same John Mark who emerges late in his life as the Gospel writer. But the statement for my sermon, while having that story clearly behind it, will not be about John Mark. Instead, my key statement will be placed in a contemporary form and will be very simple. It will be along the line that no matter how much one has failed, or thinks one has failed, at any stage of one's life there is still always time, through God's grace and help, to change, to come back. It is not as clearly stated at this point as I expect it to be, but my sense of what the sermon will say is now taking shape. I am ready to move on.

The next two steps or stages of this planning process are also interchangeable, and often one is helped by trying to work through them both somewhat simultaneously. These steps deal with, first, the formation of a controlling metaphor for the sermon, a metaphorical idea that corresponds directly to the central statement of the sermon. Second, the steps involve the gathering of materials from which the completed sermon will be fashioned. With this interchangeability in mind, we will look first at the search for a controlling metaphor—which again, it should be said, every sermon to be preached without notes should have.

Devising the Sermon's Metaphor

For any public address to be cohesive, moving, and remembered, it has to be stuctured around a metaphor, something to which the mind can attach itself. Again, when we prepare our sermons as manuscripts or as complex note systems, we tend to overlook or play down the role of metaphor. But my experience is that in sermons preached without notes, the central metaphor is often the key to how well the sermon will actually fly when it is preached. As one speaks, it is the metaphor that one conjures up. It says, in effect, "let me tell you what this idea is like" and the "like" becomes the metaphoric wing upon which ideas, thoughts, and theological notions can take off. One remembers metaphor, and if the metaphor is a good one—original, provocative, and closely aligned with what one wishes to say—then, in remembering the metaphor, one also remembers that to which the metaphor gave form and life. In homiletics and in the work of preachers, far too little time is given to the devising of fresh, luminous metaphors for sermons.

However, the fact is that one does not *find* a metaphor; one actually *creates* a metaphor. Something does not *have* metaphoric meaning; it is always *given* metaphoric meaning by the one in whose hands it will become a metaphor. And literally anything can become a metaphor. The chair in which I sit can be a metaphor—a chair that leans back too far and that may account for my occasional backaches, a chair that I dearly love, but one, I know, that sooner or later I am going to have to give up. I am describing my old chair, which is not itself a metaphor but a chair; and yet I can very easily, and with some significance, turn my old chair into a metaphor for ways of thinking and acting that go way beyond this old chair. Anything can *become* a metaphor and can be placed, often with remarkable results, at the service of the sermon. One must learn to see objects, events, simple ways of doing things, or ordinary events, for their metaphoric value. Simple descriptions can reveal and delight as metaphor. Every sermon, particularly every sermon to be preached without manuscript or notes, needs to be couched in metaphor.

At the same time that I am thinking about the bottom line of my John Mark sermon, I am also thinking about a metaphor for it. It must be a metaphor for the sermon's bottom line, as I have just stated it, not something tangential to the Mark story as I will tell it. For some reason, this does not take very long this time (even though sometimes it does). Mark came back from what I take to be a long period of trauma and regret to become a Gospel writer, to write his Gospel. That is how I will put it. Metaphorically, I will make that jump: Even today we, like Mark, should realize that no matter what we have had to live through, no matter how bad things have been in our lives, it is never too late to come back and write our own gospel. It is a simple line, but I like it. These words will become my metaphor, the metaphor this time being verbal. The sermon will be couched in that metaphoric language. Gospels are written in a lot of ways. Sometimes with pen and ink, but also sometimes with how our lives are lived. It is never too late to write one's own gospel. That will be the Mark metaphor for my sermon.

Gathering the Sermon's Materials

Thus far, then, I have the central thrust of my sermon. I have worked the series of texts that, for me, shall become the major story of the sermon, the story of John Mark. I have a sense not only of what the sermon will be about but what I want to say in it; and I have a metaphorical line—"writing a gospel"—which I will thread through the sermon. One thing, however, remains in this planning period: I must come up with other nonbiblical materials with which the sermon will be fleshed out. These materials can come from any number of sources, most of which I have discussed in other places.[2] There are four basic "barrels," though, through which the preacher should rummage at this stage. One is current events. Not just the big events that currently rivet the public's attention, but the little events, those that one finds in and should clip from the newspaper, those about the traumas and triumphs of people's lives. Another barrel is what I have called popular culture. This is not news, though it is sometimes found in newspapers. It is television, widely seen sitcoms, advertising, particular television commercials, movies, and popular books of all kinds. It is material that is a part of the larger shared culture in which we all, to a certain extent, live. One must always be careful with these materials in a sermon, since one can never assume that everyone in a congregation knows about what might be familiar to the preacher, but certain things from public consciousness, if described well, can connect with many people.

Still another barrel for such sermon material is history of all kinds. The preacher knows some history—history of a particular church, sometimes full of wild stories, the history of the Reformation, or even of one's own denomination or tradition. History can also include biography. One does not need to look very far on today's cable channels to see the degree to which people seem to be fascinated by both history and biography.

There is one other, very important, barrel from which materials for the sermon can, and should, be drawn. This is one's own personal experience. The preacher lives life as all of his or her parishioners live life: going here and there, doing a job, shopping, and enjoying family times out. The preacher is also subjected to all of the travails and troubles that all other human beings experience as well. There are car accidents and kids' injuries. There are (sometimes) overdue bills and bad decisions. What the preacher should do, though, is constantly watch and listen to those with whom he or she interacts, whether neighbors or strangers. Life is complex and its daily events are unexpected. It is those unexpected moments— moments to which the preacher, along with everyone else, is party—that present materials that enhance the sermon. I encourage my students to learn to keep a log of experiences, writing down at least one per day with enough detail to be recalled months later if need be. Preachers in their ministries should do the same. It is a discipline that serves good preachers on a regular basis. The log provides the source of the preacher's own experiences for the sermon, not with stories about the preacher—that would be too egotistical—but stories of other people, drawn from the preacher's own observation and even participation.

The last barrel of personal observation and experience is, in many ways, the most important of all of the resource materials for the sermon to be preached without notes. This is because the sermon without notes is, by its very nature, a highly personal communication experience. It is direct. It connects directly. The preacher speaks from the heart, as we put it earlier. The preacher expresses himself or herself, and it is to be expected that the preacher's own life will become, in an unobtrusive way, the ground from which the sermon arises. One will learn how important this is with the growing experience of preaching without notes.

The search at this crucial stage of the sermon is nothing more or less than brainstorming through one's notes and recollections. The method that has evolved for me is to write my topic and central sentence at the top of a sheet of paper and begin making a spontaneous list of everything I can think of from these barrels that might have any bearing whatsoever on what my sermon is about. My preference is for this list to have twelve or more items on it, several of which will be discarded as the sermon emerges. But I will not know which will be kept and which discarded until the sermon's form actually begins to emerge.

What to do? First, in assembling such a list, write down on the page everything that crosses your mind. Do not censor the process here; that will come later. Surprisingly, some ideas that may seem far-fetched at this stage turn out not to be so as the sermon evolves. Second, with your page and some note paper beside you, go deliberately from one of the barrels we just mentioned to another. As you ruminate, get up and move around, putter, giving your mind some room to move around, too, without letting it stray too intensely to other things. Third, make this list as long as you can, even though you may think you are getting too far afield. And, fourth, when you come up with an item, write it down fully enough that you can recollect it later. One word or two as a note to yourself can often get lost when you try to figure out what those words meant.

In the gathering process for my sermon on John Mark, I have clearly decided to take Mark's life in a paradigmatic fashion. Mark's overall experience can illuminate, to a certain extent, all of our lives. So I find myself looking for several different things for my list. First, I am looking at the long haul of Mark's life, the movement, as it were, from his earliest years, to the decision making that got him into such trouble with Paul, to the subsequent reconciliation with Paul that seems to have followed much later, to the crisis out of which he wrote his Gospel. Encountering Mark this way almost immediately brought back to mind a public broadcasting film I had seen a few years earlier, one that had a profound impact on me at the time. It was a BBC production called 28 Up. In it, the filmmaker began in the 1960s by selecting a group of seven-year-old children, spending time with them, and interviewing them. There were kids from various backgrounds, playing on a playground together, sitting one by one or in twos or threes on a sofa, facing the camera, and answering questions like any seven-year-old would. Then the film moved ahead seven years, and there were the same dozen or so kids. Although they were now fourteen years old, the viewer could recognize them as they were being interviewed again, following up on the questions from seven years earlier. It was remarkable. Then the film moved forward again, and there were the same kids seven years later, who were now young adults of twenty-one. The film moved forward seven years once again and there were the same adults being interviewed (a couple were missing), but now at age twenty-eight. In this award-winning British film (which now, years later, stretches with this same group to age thirty-five and, recently, to age forty-two). We had actually watched these people grow up, from childhood through adolescence into adulthood. Seeing the film gives one a sense of both the continuity and the changing dimensions of human life. I had never seen anything like it. That came to mind in contemplating the life of John Mark. I will use that, somehow, someplace, in my sermon, I think.

In the brainstorming, too, I remembered a course someplace in my past on Shakespeare, in which I had to read a number of his plays. Some really stuck with me, as they have for a lot of other people. I remembered a passage in one of the plays about the stages of a person's life, a funny passage as I recalled it. It took about fifteen minutes after locating my collected works of Shakespeare to come up with the right play and the passage itself. It is in *As You Like It*. You probably remember it, too. I wrote it down carefully in my notes:

> All the world's a stage,
> And all the men and women merely players:
> They have their exits and their entrances;
> And one man in his time plays many parts,
> His acts being seven ages. At first the infant,
> Mewling and puking in the nurse's arms.
> And then the whining school-boy, with his satchel
> And shining morning face, creeping like snail
> Unwillingly to school. And then the lover,
> Sighing like furnace, with a woeful ballad
> Made to his mistress' eyebrow. Then a soldier,

Full of strange oaths and bearded like the pard,
Jealous in honour, sudden and quick in quarrel,
Seeking the buble reputation
Even in the cannon's mouth. And then the justice,
In fair round belly with good capon lined,
With eyes severe and beard of formal cut,
Full of wise saws and modern instances;
And so he plays his part. The sixth age shifts
Into the lean and slipper'd pantaloon,
With spectacles on nose and pouch on side,
His youthful hose, well saved, a world too wide
For his shrunk shank; and his big manly voice,
Turning again toward childish treble, pipes
And whistles in his sound. Last scene of all,
That ends this strange eventful history,
Is second childishness and mere oblivion,
Sans teeth, sans eyes, sans taste, sans everything." (2.7.147-74)

I have no idea what I will do with this, but Shakespeare in a sermon always sounds to me like an elegant idea. I write it out carefully because of its possibilities. We will see what happens.

The Markan paradigm of my sermon, though, is that one makes a lot of mistakes in one's youth, in one's early life—not setbacks, but flat-out mistakes, often with serious, long-lasting consequences—and then tries to come back from them to create something good from what is often a lot of past rubble of one's own making. What I need are some stories of that paradigm in a contemporary form, if I can find any. After a good deal of thinking, I come up with five or six from my own experience—one of which reflects the rubble of my own early life, though I am not at all sure at this point if I want the sermon to be that confessional.

I also have a friend from much earlier in my life who had to cope with a rather substantial prison sentence, but whose life and family are now very close to me. I sketch a few notes to identify this as a potential sequence for the sermon. Coincidentally, I know of another person, not as close to me, who went through a similar experience after returning home from Vietnam, but who, at age thirty-three, committed suicide when nothing in life seemed to work; that one seems like the Mark story in reverse. I know a person fairly well whose struggle with drugs is still ongoing, even though we hope it is behind her. She is working day-to-day to rebuild relationships and create something good from her life. She will make it. I really believe she will. And I have a preaching student, come to seminary in midlife, who is absolutely radiant at the prospect of a life of service to God—a radiance that comes from leaving behind a long past of misery, all of which was her own making, as she acknowledges. It is several hours later, though, while doing other things, that I remember the story of a young woman I once knew who, with her boyfriend, held up a bank. They were caught and she served three years in state prison. Now her life is together. She is married with two little girls of her own, and she teaches a Sunday school class. I jot her story down as a few notes, too, though a few notes is all I need in order to tell it. I do not know what I will end up using yet, but at least I am assembling the pieces.

Something is still missing though. I am going to build the sermon around the metaphor of "writing a gospel." We can all "write a gospel," but it will be written with our lives. The question that remains is: How does one do that? The task will be one of moving from metaphor to reality without losing the metaphor. The metaphor must be given concrete substance, though. I begin making some notes about that, even though I have no intention of telling anyone "how" to do it—everybody has to work that out for himself or herself—but I will want to make some suggestions, to point some directions; those will play a very important role in the sermon that emerges from this.

I have now reached a transition point in preparing my sermon on John Mark. The pieces of it are, for the most part, in hand. I know what I am working with. Next comes the assembly, the organization of the material into a working outline. In preaching this sermon without notes, I shall not even write out a full manuscript. What I do not know yet, though, is whether I shall write out any sections of the sermon in order to clarify them in my mind. Instead, I will spend significant time on preparing a detailed outline that will provide the road map through my preached sermon.

Chapter Two

Creating the Sermon Outline: Wednesday

When the ideas and the materials for the sermon are assembled, they must then be organized and arranged. The sermon's outline must be created. In some ways, it is not only the most difficult task involved in preparing the sermon to be preached without notes, it is also the most important. Quite apart from content or theology—both of which are important—if the sermon outline works, the sermon itself will work; and the better the outline is, the better the sermon will be. The outline, in fact, is the key to both ease of memorization and sureness in delivery of the sermon preached without notes.

Creating a good working outline, one that easily lends itself to being used without notes, involves four distinct and essential tasks. We can name these as (1) isolating, (2) arranging, (3) marking, and (4) evaluating the materials with which one is working. The steps involved need to be done in that order. I will explain each of them in some detail as well as indicate criteria for evaluating the overall outline that emerges. Those criteria will be crucial as well.

Isolating the Sequences of the Sermon

The sermon to be preached without notes must be broken up into clearly marked sections or pieces. We will call these "sequences." They will be viewed as the stones from which the sermon's structure will be built. Each must be clear and distinct.

Each must be one unit of material and one only, even if that means breaking up a single large chunk into several smaller, distinct, contributing parts. This is one of the major differences between outlining the inductive sermon to be preached without notes and the older forms of sermon outlining, particularly the outlining of the deductive sermon. It used to be that one would create a series of what were considered to be large or major points and then create any number of subpoints that would handle all of the variations or lesser ideas that supported those major points. The outline would be structured in a way that virtually everyone recognizes from high school English classes:

I.
  A.
    1.
    2.
    3.
  B.
    1.
    2.
II.
  A.
    1.
      a.
      b.
    2.
  B.
  C.
III.
  A.
  B.
    1.
    2.

This, in fact, is the kind of outline that was used for years with various deductive forms of preaching. For example, in Charles

Koller's 1962 book, *Expository Preaching Without Notes,* to which I referred earlier, this is the only type of outlining recommended.[1] In the book's key illustrative sermon, based on Acts 2 and titled "The World's Most Attractive Church," the sermon's proposition is that the church "revealed" in the second chapter of Acts had a power that today's church does not have. Why? the sermon then asked. The answer was that the church described in Acts 2 had a very unique membership, one that exhibited four elements of "strength." Hence, the four main points of the sermon:

I. They were a united membership.
II. They were an informed membership.
III. They were a spiritual membership.
IV. They were a witnessing membership.

Then, under each of these four main points was a strikingly complex set of subpoints, all of which had to be memorized in order to preach the sermon without notes. For example, to take only one subset, under "They were a spiritual membership" were these three subpoints, quoted here just as they appear in Koller's sermon outline:

1. The original 120 had been "filled with the Holy Spirit" (vs. 4).
—Not like cup, half full, pathetically trying to run over.
2. The later 3000 received the Holy Spirit (vs. 38).
—Like 3000 clocks, all sizes, moved by the same current, same time.
3. The combined group were ministering in power of Holy Spirit. . . .
—Nothing so attractive as real spirituality—can't remain "small but spiritual."

Materials are arranged the same way under each of the four main headings of the sermon's body. Between the main point about spiritual membership and the three subpoints, the amount of barely connected material is almost overwhelming, posing not only an enormous challenge to memorization, but also to listener comprehension when the material is actually spoken. The problem with this outline is not so much its material as its sheer complexity. The outlining that we are proposing here for the inductive sermon without notes seeks to create and capitalize on simplicity. It is not oversimplistic, as we shall discover when we get to the memorizing phase, but it seeks clarity by simplifying. In the hectic times in which preachers today do their work, simplifying becomes an enormous gift. So, in everything we do from the beginning to the ending of our sermon, we are going to simplify. The outline is one of the major places where we are able to do so.

Our sermon, in short, will not be constructed as a traditional outline. It will be a sequential arrangement of isolated, blocked-out materials. It will contain anywhere from seven or eight to as many as ten or twelve sequences, each one making its own unique contribution to the unfolding of what we want the sermon ultimately to say. Materials, usually explanatory, will be lodged within (or under) each of the sequences; these will sometimes be materials familiar to the preacher, thus requiring little memory work, but sometimes, as we shall see, they will require memorization. This will all become clearer and less daunting as we proceed.

I can now start to isolate the various pieces of sermon material I assembled in chapter one in order to build my outline. I have worked through the John Mark story, and it is relatively complex. So I am going to simplify it by breaking it down into several sequences, each of which will stand on its own in my memory even though they will flow together when I tell the story. I have Mark's early life, both as textual notes about where he lived and who he knew, and as speculative ideas about the reference in Mark's Gospel to the "young man." For now, that early life will be one sequence—a sequence of who he was, where he came from, and what we know or can guess about his youth. Next I have the story of Mark's going to Antioch with Paul and Barnabas and the experience of that first missionary trip with them—the story, in effect, of his desertion, passed over without comment at this point in the Acts story. That is detailed enough to be a sequence: the desertion sequence.

Then, I skip to the second trip and the bitter breakdown between Paul and Barnabas, all because of Mark; they part company, Barnabas taking Mark and going back home to Cyprus and who knows where, and Paul selecting a new partner, Silas. Acts constructs their travel from that point on. It is a remarkable sequence, but I want it to stand alone as far as my outlining is concerned. I want to be able to give it all of the drama that it deserves. After that, I will jump ahead a number of years and there is Paul in prison, writing his letters, mentioning John Mark. So what happened? Here I will enjoy the imaginative process. Did Paul realize how harsh he had been and get in touch with Mark? Did Mark realize what a foolish mistake he had made, whether intentional or not, and send a letter of apology to Paul? Would that we knew. A sequence is there, a strong one; Paul and John Mark are finally together again, but how?

Finally, around the year 65 Paul is martyred, the Romans move on Palestine, on Jerusalem, and the Temple and everything else is destroyed. Someone must write an account of the Christ, something that pulls together old writings and records, the letters of Paul, and accounts of Jesus' teaching. And there, amid the tragedy, John Mark steps up. This forms another sequence. The Gospel is written. It speaks to people, Christians and non-Christians alike, scattered the world over.

So how many sequences has the expanded text actually given me? Five, if I count them correctly. They provide a way, first, for me to learn the story easily and quickly, but they also provide a way for me to tell a very disjointed story clearly and dramatically; most important, they provide a way for congregants to hear the story clearly and forcefully. To those five sequences, however, I will add others that I have collected. I have *28 Up;* I have Shakespeare's speech from *As You Like It;* I have my own story of huge mistakes I made as a young adult, and my somehow surviving them; I have several pieces—I will narrow them to three for now—of stories about people I know who have survived their own mistakes to at least begin creating lives of commitment to other people, to high ideals, to God; they have begun to "write their gospels" too. And, for now, I have a list of about five ways in which one actually can write a gospel today. Each of my five items—I shall also cut this from five to probably three—will form a separate sequence in my outline. I have my pieces now, all fourteen of them, once I've cut the last five to three. Does this mean my sermon will have fourteen points? In a sense, it does. But I am not finished paring them down yet either. The fact remains that by the time I am ready to preach, there will probably be fewer than fourteen.

Arranging the Sequences

In my experience with outlining to preach without notes, the process can seem relatively easy, but sometimes, getting the pieces into a logical, well-connected working arrangement is a struggle. Still, the time and effort it calls for is more than worth it in the final outcome. Here, there are choices to be made, even though with this sermon on John Mark the pieces seem to fall fairly easily into place. The key questions are, first, What comes at the beginning and the end of the sermon? and, second, Should the sequences of biblical text—in this case, my five Mark sequences—be kept together or broken up through the sermon? Since my sermon has no text, as such, I will open with the Mark sequences; in other words, I will begin by telling the story of John Mark, using my sequences as a clearly laid out guide for the telling. Without actually saying so, I will tell the Mark story as a series of takes in my mind. I will introduce these sequences by saying that I intend to share a

Bible story that is not often told because one must, in a sense, sleuth it out. But I shall sleuth it out here for the telling. Come along with me.

Sequence six, after the five on Mark, will be the *28 Up* piece. I will explain what the film is and what it does and will assume that no one except me has seen it. I am able, I think, to explain the film well enough, and briefly enough, so that everyone will feel its sense of impact as I have. I will also explain how, like the story of Mark, the film enables us to become aware of our lives not as an event here or there, but through a long lens; we see others (again like Mark) from childhood into adulthood. We become conscious of the contours of our lives, the eras through which we live. We see ourselves as having a biography that, looking back, we are able to trace.

For some reason, I become aware at this point that even though I like the idea of using the Shakespeare speech in this sermon, it is going to be too much. If I did not have the *28 Up* sequence, I would probably use it here in its place, but I am ready to make the difficult decision (for me) that the Shakespeare piece is out. I will not use it this time.

Sequences seven, eight, and nine, then, will be three brief stories of people I know—people whose lives, looking back, were contoured much like John Mark's. I have made the decision to leave my own life out of the sermon. While my life fits the Mark model, which is why I can so empathize with Mark in this sermon, to bring myself into it would be too personally intrusive. I will not name my three friends, but I will briefly sketch the predicament, the problem, the failure—I am not sure what to even call it yet—that each one created early on in life. Then each one, in the language of Jesus' parable of the prodigal son, came to himself or herself, and the struggle for transformation began. Each sequence will be told briefly, sketched by a few details. I want to bring the Mark story from the past into the present. Each of the three wants more than anything else to "write a gospel" now, as I will try to thread that metaphor through the sermon.

My last three sequences will mark the transition to how one writes that gospel. I should say that I am one who believes that preaching, at least in the time emerging ahead of us, needs to be proactive. By that, I mean that the sermon should deliberately and consciously make behavioral suggestions. There was a time, years ago, when homileticians talked about ending sermons with what was called "application"; that is, "Now that I have explained or expounded the Bible text, how do we apply it in our lives?" Then came the inductive sermon and with it the idea that everyone who heard the sermon should find in it whatever they would for themselves; sermons should just end, or end with a question. No two people could or would take the same thing away from the sermon, and the preacher should not try to tamper with that. Preach provocatively or biblically, and then stop. Leave it to the hearers to fill in the ending or the application.

Over the last several years, however, we have begun to sense, I think, that ending the sermon this way leaves hearers more in a quandary than in a searching mode. Those who share the sermon, more often than not, are puzzled or even perplexed at being left on their own. This is not to say that they want preachers telling them what to do at the sermon's end—that is a far end of the pendulum's swing. But neither do they want preachers leaving them dangling at the end—that is the other end of the pendulum's swing. They come toward the end of a good sermon, instead, with an unspoken query: "What do you think I should do, now that I have heard your sermon? I like what you have said, but now give me some ideas about what I might do with it." That is where the good sermon brings the hearers. And it is *that* which the preacher should hear and respond to in the last sequence or sequences of the sermon. It is closer to the middle of the pendulum's two directions. So the effective preacher makes some suggestions. The preacher moves the hearers in some directions—not *a* direction, but in some *possible* directions. In my judgment, this is most effective when they are behavioral directions. That is: "Here are some things that you might consider doing as a result of what we have talked about today. You might try this. Or, you might try another approach." The preacher is directive and suggestive, probing and challenging, but in a gentle, searching sort of way—for himself or herself, as well as for the congregants.

Is this true for *all* sermons? One does not want to be caught talking about all of this or that, since there are clear exceptions to any general notion. But, as far as I am concerned, it is fair to say that, while one seeks variety in addressing this in the sermon, every sermon should give rise to some clear behavioral directions. It is the equivalent of what one often finds in Jesus' parables—a clean story followed by a "go, thou, and do likewise." In our case, however, it is sometimes difficult for hearers, even keen, thoughtful ones, to know how to live out what the preacher has discussed; so it becomes the preacher's responsibility, I suggest, to offer some ways of "doing likewise," as metaphorical as that can be, as a part of every sermon.

It is not quite enough, in other words, for me to say in my sermon, "go, thou, and write your gospel." I like both the idea and the fact that, in the context of a sermon, I think I can make the idea soar. But those who share the sermon, and who might soar with that metaphoric notion, have a right to ask: How do you think we can write a gospel of our own? We cannot do what Mark did, so what can we do in writing "our" gospel? And my responsibility as preacher, after I come down from the soaring metaphor, is to offer some suggestions, which is what my last three sequences will do.

Each of my suggestions is a separate sequence in my outline. One writes a gospel by how one actually treats other people on a day-to-day basis. Surely no one thinks this goes without saying in the pulpit. How is one to treat other people, strangers in Wal-Mart, the waitress in the coffee shop, the coworker who is often an absolute pain, or even the person in the next car on the crowded freeway? One treats them all with gentleness and kindness, deliberately so. It is what the apostle Paul called the "fruits of the Spirit," the simple graces of life and love.

One writes a gospel by the use of one's resources, one's money. Generosity, done with simplicity and humility, becomes a basis for how one lives life. One is not greedy, not miserly, not stingy. One does not live as though looking out, always, for Number One. Number One, in fact, is the Other Person, often the person in need, however or wherever one encounters that person. Such things do not go without saying. This kind of life, actualized on a day-to-day basis in one's dealings, forms the materials from which a gospel is written today.

Finally, one writes a gospel by faithfulness within a community of faith, whatever that community is. And since I am preaching this sermon within this congregation of faith, I have no qualms advocating that one write one's gospel by faithfulness *here,* in *this* church. Can one be a good Christian and not be faithful in worship and congregational connectedness? Yes, perhaps. At least I do not want to say unequivocally that one cannot. Can one write a visible, compelling gospel with one's life and not be faithful within a family of faith? No, at least not in my view. That, too, is important if one is really intent on writing a gospel with one's life.

Marking the Sequences

My sequences, now, are arranged. They have an order. But there is a third step in the process, one of marking or labeling the sequences. The farther the sermon moves toward the moment of preaching, the more important this step becomes. One must create a set of simple titles, one for each sequence. They must be precise and clear. They must say in a couple of words exactly what the sequence involves. They are important because it is these titles that will be commited to memory as a basis for preaching the sermon without notes. What we are making here is a list of carefully structured items, items clearly marked and easily remembered.

My own experience is that such things as acrostics and alliteration are of little value in making these lists or in the sermons preached from them. Acrostics are lists of things, the first letters of which spell out a word; for example, M-O-T-H-E-R, with M standing for "More and Better Things," O standing for "Otherwise One Should Punt," T standing for "Try Harder If Necessary," and so on. Alliteration refers to a list of items with the first word of each item beginning with the same letter; that is, every first word in the list begins with E. We are inclined to think that these are aids for remembering things in a list, and if one is learning an abstract list, they probably can help. But for sermons of the kind we have in mind, they are little, if any, help. I suggest that one not even try such things; they can quickly become much too cute and gimmicky. Several things bear on this. First, the memorizing that we will focus on later depends not on gimmicks, but on creating a strong logic and connectedness of our sequential arrangement. One may incorrectly assume that, at this point, memorizing is not the problem that it is. Second, the tricks like acrostic are often designed so that hearers of the list can remember it as well. The fact is that, in our sermons, we are not very concerned that congregants remember our sequential list. Our concern, instead, is that they catch where the list is taking them, where it ends up.

Nor is it necessary or even desirable in the inductive sermon that sequences be labeled in perfect parallel fashion, as in Koller's four marks of the church in Acts 2: It was a "united" church, an "informed" church, a "spiritual" church and a "witnessing" church. In fact, since we are constructing a list of eight to ten or more sequences as our outline, it is virtually impossible for us to make the formation of each title parallel with all of the others. Even to try would waste too much time and serve little useful purpose. What one learns very quickly in doing this is that memorization depends no more on parallelism than it does on arrangements by acrostic or alliteration. Memorization depends on the connectedness of the items in the list, as well as on the ways in which each item, by its own logic, opens the door to the next.

There are times, in fact, when one wants a series of sequences to appear unrelated to one another as they are laid out in the sermon. It is like hanging strings side by side on a clothesline, strings that at first have nothing to do with each other. Then, toward the end, the pieces, the strings, begin to connect. Some principle of commonality emerges that ties them all together. It gives one the feeling of reading a good detective story when that happens, when the pieces fall into place. One will memorize the titles of the carefully crafted sequences, but each one will appear to be a sequence unto itself until some point later in the sermon when they all begin to converge. It is a truly exciting thing when that kind of logic is achieved in public address.

I will now try to construct the titles, the identity markers, of the sequences in my John Mark sermon. My first set of working notes looks like this:

1. John Mark's boyhood: What do we know?
2. John Mark as a young adult: Trust and Desertion
3. The breakup of Paul and Barnabas over John Mark
4. Late in life: Paul and John Mark back together, but how?
5. Tragedy strikes Jerusalem/Palestine, and John Mark writes his Gospel (the metaphor)
6. See life through the long lens: 28 Up
7. Overcoming early failure: Tom from prison to ministry with inmates
8. Overcoming, again: Jennie's long trip out of prison life
9. Overcoming: From early rebellion against church to commitment to service
10. Write gospel by serving others with kindness/gentleness
11. Write gospel by resources
12. Write gospel by presence in community of faith

This outline, however, is far from finished. It is not even ready yet for the memorization process to begin. The whole thing must now be tested and refined. It must be thought through, piece by piece, gone over carefully to see if, or how well, it holds together. It is time to look critically at the overall arrangement and cohesion of what I am planning to preach.

Evaluating the Outline

At this point, we are backing away from the sequences somewhat in order to think through the overall sermon. We have in mind three criteria for this critical evaluation of what we have done so far—and we will try to disassociate ourselves as much as possible from the sermon's construction so that we can see it as dispassionately and critically as possible.

We are looking, first, at the sermon's *unity*. Do the sequences hold together? Do they hold together in the order in which I have placed them? How will the transitions from one sequence to another need to be made? As I think from one sequence to the next, is there a logical and workable transition that easily makes each connection? Does the sermon have a good beginning and ending? In deliberately thinking through my list, I gradually become aware that something is seriously wrong with my outline of sequences. It goes from feeling that something is not quite right here to having to isolate what that might be. My first clue is that the transition from sequence five to six is not an easy one. The connection wants to be from five to seven, from John Mark's story to stories that I know, stories that, in a sense, are today's versions of John Mark's ordeal. That means that *28 Up* has to be moved in order for that jump to be made in the most natural way. I like *28 Up*, and I want it to play a critical role in the sermon.

At the same time, though, I have come to believe that the beginning of the sermon—jumping in with John Mark—is not as strong up front as it might be. I decide to try *28 Up* at the beginning of the sermon. I will begin (I think) in the present, tell the 28 Up story first, create a brief recognition transition, and use it to move into the story of John Mark. I will, in fact, use the 28 Up piece as a way to get my congregants looking at their own lives from the outset. From there, then, we will go back to the John Mark story and the stages of his life from age seven to fourteen to twenty-one to twenty-eight and onward. Having done that, then, I can move directly from John Mark's coming back to write his Gospel to the call to those whom I have seen in my time who come back from negative situations to write their gospels, too. Not that their gospels are already written; some are still (like a stage of John Mark's life) making ready to write a gospel; while others are already writing. That is the way my mind is carrying out this rehearsal of the outline that has already undergone some significant change.

The second thing to look for in evaluating, or rehearsing, the outline is *variety* in the sequences that make up the sermon. By variety, though, I mean something specific. That is, every sequence must make its own unique contribution to the overall sermon. Sequences should not duplicate one another. If two or more sequences do the same thing, or say the same thing, or even make the same point, they will be redundant in the final sermon. It does not take much time looking over my sermon's sequences for me to realize that sequences seven, eight, and nine are almost mirror images. If I should tell all three of those stories, however briefly, they would sound virtually alike, and the sharpness of the very point itself would be lost. Nor can the three stories be rolled together in any way. That would become too mushy and generic. I am faced, I know, with selecting one of those three sequences, or stories, and letting that one stand for the others as well. For various reasons, I will pick the Jennie story and will fill it out a bit more than I had originally planned. It will provide a kind of parable of all of us contemporary John Marks. We all made those mistakes, those errors, those failures of trust, those desertions, and, for more of us than we think, those early experiences proved well-nigh disastrous. But no matter what these mistakes were, we, like John Mark, like Jennie, can come back, whatever we have had to do, whatever we have yet to do.

Sequences ten, eleven, and twelve are all related, but quite different, and since I will treat them fairly briefly, I can leave them intact for now. They *do* represent variety, in a way, that the three stories of seven, eight, and nine do not. At this point as well, I am able to get a sense of the transitions that will be necessary in moving from one sequence to another—at least at a few places. Not every jump from one sequence to another will require a conscious transition. The only thing needed here, to borrow from movie parlance, is a cut; that is, an ending of one sequence, an ever so slight pause, and the beginning of the next. I know, though, that a transition will be needed from the *28 Up* sequence to John Mark's boyhood. The Mark sequences will flow together without noticeable break, so no transitions are needed. No transition will be needed either between the last John Mark sequence (six) and the Jennie sequence; a break will do nicely. But a "so what" transition is called for between Jennie and sequence eight, a "So what do we do about all this, anyway?" And no transitions will be needed between the last three sequences. So my new, revised sermon outline at this point is pretty much together:

1. *28 Up*—implicates us all (transition)
2. John Mark's boyhood: What do we know?
3. John Mark as a young adult: Trust and Desertion
4. The breakup of Paul and Barnabas over John Mark
5. Late in life: Paul and John Mark back together, but how?
6. Tragedy, and John Mark steps up to write his Gospel.
7. Remember Jennie: The John Mark paradigm is still with us (transition: so what now?)
8. We still overcome to write a gospel: By lives of kindness and gentleness.

9. Still write gospel: By handling of our resources

10. Still write gospel: By presence in faith community

So now I have ten sequences instead of twelve. The sermon seems tighter, more compact. There is a third important criterion that I apply at this stage to my sermon outline. This is used more as a way to sharpen the sermon than to alter it, as I did with the other two criteria. This is the criterion that I call *flow*. Does the sermon flow well, or, put another way, does it move well? In this sense, the sermon should be viewed as itself a story. One is going to preach it without notes, and, in doing so, one is going to be telling the sermon as one tells a good story. Each sequence in the sermon, from this vantage point, becomes a kind of chapter in the story. There are breaks in the story, places where the overall story stops and changes gears, where we pick it up at a different place, or double back to pick up someplace where the story left off. These breaks do not coincide with all of the sequences, but we need to be aware of where they are so that the flow can build with them, through them, and even around them.

For example, I now see the *28 Up* piece as setting up a kind of framework for the entire sermon. Everybody's life will be looked at through the *28 Up* lens—John Mark's, Jennie's, mine, and yours. So we become part of that film. We each look back and wonder about what we were like at seven and fourteen and twenty-eight; and we wonder what titles might be given to the decades past of our lives. Go ahead, think about your own life like *28 Up*. It is a potent paradigm from which the sermon is now ready to flow.

Then sequences two, three, four, five, and six are a whole piece, broken down into discrete sequences for my memorizing, but not for the telling. The story of John Mark will flow without interruption. There will be a shift, a statement of transition, between Mark's writing of his Gospel and the story of Jennie.

There will be another transitional shift, then, after Jennie's story, a place to reflect on the fact that most of us have never been to prison, and we certainly did not desert Paul, but we know that experience of failure. However we know it, we still know it. No matter what we have been, no matter what we did in the past, we begin again. We fix things. We patch them up. We pray. We pull ourselves back together. We find people willing to help us. And, with God's grace, we start over. Many are in the process of starting over; the decision to do so is already made. We are John Mark. The world needs a lot of gospel, and we are called to write our own. Here. Now. It will be read if we write it. We know that.

But how do we write one? And here another take, probably the most important—and visible—one in the sermon. We will ask the question: How? One can only suggest some ways in which gospels are still being written. Then I add my three concluding sequences, woven together as three suggestions. It is my ending. It is low-key. It is action oriented. It expects those who share the words to do something. The sermon does have the flow now that I want it to have; when I preach it without notes, I am able to tell it like a story, speeded up at some points, slowed down at others, filled with details in some parts, but filled with curiosity and questioning at others. It is a story, overall, that implicates us all, that arises directly from Christian Scripture, as I want it to, and that has a satisfying ending—not a closed ending, but one that requires something of us all—again, as I want it to.

Amplifying the Outline

I am now happy, I think, with the outline. I will still tinker with it until time to preach it. However, one thing remains for me to do, even though I have gradually been doing it all along the way. I still need to fill in details that I will have to know—details that I will be expected to memorize—under each of my sequences. I emphasize that I am "expected to memorize" these details since for some of the sequences I know the materials fairly well already. I will rehearse in my mind the stories of Jennie and *28 Up*, both things that I can create fairly easily; and in the last three sequences I know pretty much what I plan to say. My comments there will be personal, suggestive only, and fairly short. It will be my heart speaking there, since my suggestions represent things in which I believe very deeply. I will need a few notes on sequence one: *28 Up*. I am going to look up who made the movie and when it was begun, information that I think I can find and commit to memory. Other than that, I think I can tell the story of what the movie was about and what its power was, and still is, as far as I am concerned.

Early on in chapter 1 of this book, I pointed out that when one plans to preach without notes, one must give extra careful attention to note taking, especially when it concerns the biblical materials on which one's sermon is built. These sequences of text—numbers two, three, four, five, and six—are the places where I have some significant materials to fill in, textual materials that I will have to know from memory. So at this point I transfer my textual notes—or at least the ones I know now that I will use—from my note cards to their place under the appropriate sequences of my outline. When we get to the next stage of work, the next chapter on memorizing, I will confront the textual notes directly and fully that, at this point, I am writing into my outline. Once the notes are transferred, my outline for preaching is (I still say it somewhat tentatively) ready.

It is at this stage, though, and this stage only, that I am ready as well to think about what my sermon will be entitled. I have come to the view over many years that sermon titles are very important. Careful thought should be given to the title. Too often, sermon titles are throwaways—too hackneyed, too clichéd, too theological, too ambiguous, too cute, too nonsensical. The sermon title ought to do several things. First, it ought to be precise as to its reflection of the sermon; it should capture the essence of the sermon, some element at the sermon's very core. Second, the title should, at the same time, withhold what the sermon is actually going to say. One should not, in other words, hear the sermon's bottom line in the title. A kind of mystery about the sermon should be held out by the title, something that causes people, after hearing the sermon and only at that point, to look back and say, "So *that's* why it was given that particular title." Finally, the title should be a lure, a fishhook of sorts, to cause a person, just on hearing the title, to think that maybe he or she should try to hear what the preacher is going to say. I have an idea about a title at this point, but I will think it over some more before I assign it for publication in bulletin or newspaper.

Chapter Three

Memorizing the Sermon Outline: Thursday and Friday

The major reason most preachers give for preaching with manuscript or detailed notes is that they would never otherwise be able to remember what they had prepared. They do not, in other words, trust their ability to memorize. Yet all of us know, though we rarely stop to acknowledge, that the human mind is a remarkable thing. Of course we all forget things, and we even tend to be haunted about things we sometimes forget. Yet the mental capacities with which we all remember, collate, use, and then store away a thousand pieces of information a day are not even fully understood. What is particularly striking about this, in fact, is that none of us in our entire educational lives is ever trained in the cultivation and enhancement of our memories. Think what would happen if we actually *practiced* remembering, if we really worked at sharpening our memory skills. That is what good speakers do.

The ability to remember is an innate human trait; remembering well is cultivated, especially by preachers who undertake to deliver their sermons every Sunday, week in and week out, without notes. In this chapter, I shall discuss the process of how memory works, based on a growing body of research, and how the preacher can develop lifelong memory skills that will pay off with dramatically better sermons. Then I will illustrate how those skills actually work by devising the plan for memorizing the materials for my sermon on John Mark.

The study of human memory, as well as the first conscious

efforts to improve it, arose, as so many things like this did, from the Greeks. The first types of what are called mnemonics—a word that refers to memory aids—were devised by the great Greek philosophers and rhetoricians. Public speech and persuasion were at the heart of Greek culture and learning, and the arts of memory, and memorization, were crucial to those arts. There is evidence that Aristotle gave Alexander the Great lessons in both rhetoric and mnemonics. While the Greeks certainly understood the importance of memorization, most of what they taught seems simplistic by contemporary gestalt standards of research and understanding. Generally, the Greek rhetoricians believed that they could isolate a single set of mnemonic devices with which all memory problems could be solved. The closest that they came was in understanding the role of repetition in improving the human mind's ability to remember.

Over the past hundred years, however, the study of human memory has become both intense and relatively scientific. The twentieth century's research has taught us basically two things. First, it has taught us just how complex and multifaceted the dynamic of human memory is; and, second, it has taught us the range of the basic components that affect both our ability to remember and our penchant for forgetting.

At the heart of this newly discovered complexity of human memory is an appreciation that we have within us not one capacity for memory, but actually two. These two capacities are long-term and short-term memory. Ironically, short-term memory is usually referred to as primary memory with long-term memory called secondary. That is not what is important, however. What is important is the difference between the two. Long-term memory is our ability to remember things from our pasts, our experiences from long ago, from childhood right on through our adult years. These are things that we call back, that sometimes we try to call back but cannot, or cannot call back very well. They are not—and this is crucial—things that we actually *tried* to remember. We just do, and we savor those long-term, or long-ago, memories.

Short-term memory, though, is different. It is the ability to remember things that we try, overtly and consciously, to remember. It is studying to remember. It is working at remembering something that, for a particular time and place, we need to remember. That is short-term memory—primary memory. We study for a test using our short-term, or primary, memory; we prepare for a driver's exam, and we study the driving manual, trying to remember what the speed limit is in a school zone, or which lanes we can or cannot make left turns from. These things represent conscious work at remembering, sometimes successful, sometimes not. On some occasions, things that were learned as part of one's short-term memory become part of one's long-term memory as well—though not necessarily so. It is also true, as we will become aware, that elements from our long-term memory, from our past, also have a bearing from time to time on how well our short-term memories work.[1]

For our purposes, this distinction is very important, since the memory we need to enhance for preaching without notes is, clearly, short-term memory. We need to be able to learn specific things well in the course of two to three days at most, recall those things easily and accurately, and then, remarkably, we need for that short-term memory to actually fade just as quickly as it came. That, in fact, is one of the advantages of good short-term memory. What we learn and remember for a short time disappears as quickly as we learned it. For the preacher, this means that after the sermon is preached, it is time to begin the next sermon, so one needs for the memorized material of that preceding sermon to disappear, to get out of the way in order that it not cloud the emergence of the new sermon material that must now take over the short-term memory. It really is remarkable the way that this process works.

We need to begin, though, by understanding the five factors that contemporary research has shown to contribute to good short-term memory. After that, I will note three things that interfere with short-term memory, or with the process of making it work. Then we will turn to the memorization of our sermon outline for preaching about John Mark.

Good Physical, Mental Health

First, relatively new research has demonstrated the relationship that exists between good physical and mental health and the keenness of short-term memory. Since remembering is a function of the brain, any kind of poor health, fatigue, pain, or even physical discomfort affects the brain's performance. By the same token, any kind of mental or emotional distress, or just plain stress, takes its toll on the ability of the brain to work at its full capacity. One must be well rested, alert, and properly functioning both during the work of memorizing and in the moment of publicly recalling what one has memorized. Moreover, the memorization cannot be done late at night or during any other period when one's brain is tired. Nor can one expect to preach a sermon without notes very well when one is physically tired; again, one's brain will not do a very good job of remembering what it is expected, and even trained, to do.

Interest in the Material

Second, research of various kinds (as if we did not know it before) has also made it clear that there is a direct and powerful relationship between one's interest in material and the ease with which one memorizes it. What we are interested in, our minds are already in sync with; what we are deeply interested in, our minds seem to siphon up. What does this say to the preacher? Does it mean that you should preach only those things, or about those things, in which you are deeply interested, since only those things lend themselves to efficient memorization and thus to being preached without notes? I am not suggesting that at all. What this *should* mean, however, is that whatever the subject or the material to be addressed in the sermon, you should seek to bring your own interests into a full and lively interaction with that subject. The preacher, in other words, should find in the material being addressed his or her keenest point of interest and devise a sermon that reflects where the preacher stands vis-à-vis the topic. In that way, the preacher's interest level is, in fact, piqued at making this point of the sermon, and what results will be a sermon that not only engages the preacher, but because of that engagement, also lends itself to relatively easy memorization.

Ironically, it is true that one hears many sermons in which the preacher seems to have relatively little interest. One can hear this not only in the words and ideas that come from the pulpit, but even more in how they are expressed. It is also true that, when one preaches, congregants will experience no higher level of interest in the sermon than they detect in the one delivering the sermon. The reverse is the case, as well: When the preacher's level of interest and involvement in the sermon is high, when it is backed by passion, then that high level of interest, involvement, and passion will be picked up and shared by those who experience the sermon. Somewhat contrary to what we said a moment ago, there may be a rare occasion when the preacher should probably avoid a sermon topic or text in which he or she has no interest whatsoever and cannot conjure up any such interest. Still, the rule is that, for both ease of memorization for preaching and as a concern for the well-being of one's congregants, the preacher should bring to the pulpit only those topics and issues that have, indeed, stirred a significant intensity of interest in the preacher's heart.

The Need for Concentration

Third, it is axiomatic that short-term memorization depends, to an enormous extent, on one's focusing keen attention, or concentration, on what is being learned. This means that one must work in circumstances that do not allow the mind to wander. Everyone knows the experience of reading a page of something and afterward having no immediate memory at all of what was on the page. One's eyes were working, but the mind was somewhere else, and we came out of the reading with absolutely nothing. One rereads the page, this time telling oneself to keep one's mind on the material at hand.

Short-term memorization depends on being active and alert, even intensely so, during the memorization process. It means finding a place where one literally can shut out everything else for an hour or two, not only to be uninterrupted, but also to be undistracted for a period of time. It does work that several short periods of time—say, a half hour at various intervals—can serve just as well for this period of intense concentration. The issue is alertness and focus, all deliberately and consciously activated. I have learned from hard experience that this cannot, for me at least, be done in my office or even in my study. For me in sermon memorization, it is best done (when weather permits) outdoors, out behind my shed under a tree that I like a lot. There I have privacy, and I can walk around, sit on a nearby stump when I want to, or talk aloud unself-consciously in ways that I certainly do not want others to hear. An hour under my tree, fully awake, feeling good, and I can have a sermon outline fairly well memorized. This clearly amounts to a suspension of time so that one's undivided attention and concentration can be *only* on the material being memorized. When this time is worked on a regular basis, as a firmly established routine of time and place, memorizing the outline and materials for a sermon becomes as normal, natural, and even pleasurable an experience as one can imagine.

Clear, Concise Organization

The fourth dimension of this memorizing process has already been done, even though its full importance can only be highlighted here. The week so far has been spent in preparing the sermon and in fashioning it into a working outline. Of all the things that recent research has taught us about the enhancement of human memory, none is more important than the clear, concise organization of the materials to be memorized. Disjointed materials, of whatever kind, are very difficult to handle in short-term memory. Materials that are unrelated to one another, or that *seem* unrelated because their levels of abstraction are so high, are difficult to both memorize and recall. The human mind needs order for it to do its work of remembering—not any particular order, or some cosmic order, but its own order. This means that what may seem orderly to one person may appear very disorderly, or disorganized, to someone else. But, for everyone, in order for memory to work most efficiently, the materials one seeks to memorize must be perceived to be in a logical, well-connected arrangement. The order must, in other words, be fully, consciously visible to the one doing the memorization. For this to be the case, memory researchers have come to use a strange term to talk about arranging and setting up materials for memorizing. They call the process "chunking." As one scholar puts it, "The unit used to measure primary memory capacity is usually a *chunk*. A chunk is a unit of information organized according to a rule or corresponding to some familiar pattern."[2]

Does that sound familiar? What we have done in our approach to sermon outlining in the previous chapter amounts to a kind of "chunking." We have carved out blocks of information or ideas for the sermon, lining them up according to a pattern that, from the material, seems logical. We learn in chunks. Each of our sequences, in this sense, is a chunk, and from those chunks, our sermon is built. Now, we memorize the chunks, and we are able to do it with ease because we have spent careful time planning and evaluating in order to form the chunks (or sequences) into the whole of our sermon. We have, in effect, constructed an outline for preaching precisely along the lines that are most conducive to memorizing it for the pulpit.

Repetition and Memory

A fifth and final element goes into this process of short-term memorization of the sermon outline. It is not only the final element, it is also the original one, the one that the Greeks first taught us. It is the process of repetition. There is no substitute for it. What we have indicated thus far is that human memory, particularly short-term or primary memory, is significantly aided by a number of well-documented factors: good health (both physical and mental), interest, intense concentration, and the organization of material. But those things do not actually produce the short-term memorization. They enhance it or make it possible; they make it easy and reachable. Only the repetition of the materials to be memorized, within the context of those factors, actually results in activating short-term memory.

Some memory scholars refer to this repetitive process as "rehearsal." Scholars also tell us that this use of repetition, or rehearsal, in order to commit chunks of material to memory is itself a learned process, since there is no evidence that children do it either naturally or innately. There is a rote quality to such repetition, to be sure, but when the factors of attention and clear organization of material are present, the rote process is not nearly as mechanical as it sounds. With repetition, over an hour or two of concentration, or even over three or four half-hour periods, the materials become etched fairly easily within one's mind—an etching that will, with some slight freshening, last for several days.

For me, with the Mark sermon that I am preparing here, the repetitive process will focus on two different things. First, I will repeat again and again the outline of the sermon itself— my ten sequences and the couple of transitions I need. I will rehearse the sequential outline thoroughly until I know the "chunks" in order. The few transitions will come easily after I know the sequences. I will then spend time learning by repetition the fleshed out material of the sermon's content; particularly, in this case, the Mark material that I will sketch in detail—as it is in my notes—shortly. In this case, I will pay special attention to knowing the precise biblical texts and the details of the Markan story. I will work on this material separately, however, until the last half-hour or so when I will go through it all, more or less, together. Each person will have to develop his or her own habits for this repetitive routine, and my experience with students is that it differs somewhat from person to person.

One question that comes up is whether such repetition should be done covertly or overtly, that is, whether it should be in one's head or spoken aloud. The answer is both. My preference, for the most part, is for working aloud, speaking so that I can hear myself—which, of course, is why I prefer to do the work outdoors, out behind my shed under the tree. No one can hear me there. Rehearsing or repeating the sequences and the materials aloud does two things. First, it assists me in maintaining concentration. I cannot have a wandering mind when I am forcing myself to repeat the sequences aloud. Second, doing this enables me to get the feel for what the words sound like as I say them. I am not studying for a test in which I shall quietly sit and write down the answers as they pop into my head; I am, instead, preparing to speak aloud everything that I am now memorizing. So, I am doing more than just repeating for the sake of memorizing my outline; I am actually rehearsing what I am going to say at the same time that I memorize it.

I can and do go over and over in my head what I am memorizing, often as a way of refreshing what I have worked on. One can do this anywhere, of course, and I often use time sitting alone—in a doctor's office, in the car waiting to pick someone up, in the early morning over some cups of strong coffee—to work on my memorization. It is time well spent. I usually do it covertly as well for fifteen or twenty minutes as soon as I arrive at the church on Sunday morning, often sitting in the sanctuary for one last run-through.

Interferences with Short-Term Memory

It is important to go a step beyond this, however, taking account of the fact that there are several factors that can interfere with short-term memory, even after one has learned what one set out to learn. These can be overcome by some combination of the five factors that we have just discussed, but even this is made easier if one is aware of the forms that "interference," as memory scholars call it, can take.

First, *events* that take place between memorizing and the time for recall can interfere with how well the recall takes place. When one learns well the sermon outline and its supporting material for Sunday morning, but then experiences something traumatic on Saturday afternoon or evening, one's recall of even that well-memorized sermon outline can be affected. Depending on the degree to which the event disrupts the mental and emotional state of the preacher, he or she may need to make adjustments in order to preach the sermon without notes as planned. Sometimes, this adjustment will amount to no more than the preacher actively staying focused on the sermon, compartmentalizing a particular event's emotional impact to a part of one's mind for the time being; it may also mean that the preacher spends some additional time rehearsing, both overtly and covertly, the outline that was earlier memorized in preparation for preaching. A preacher must have an awareness of the way in which such interference works in order to determine what adjustments are needed to preach most effectively without notes.

Second, what is sometimes called *prior learning*—ideas that one holds from the past, usually deeply emotional ideas—can cause interference with one's memorization in the present. This is not easy to overcome, even though sometimes it becomes necessary to try to do so. It is not that one cannot work through and absorb new ideas or ways of looking at things as part of sermon preparation. Often, in fact, this is one of the most interesting aspects of preparing sermons on a weekly basis: it keeps one's mind fresh and moving, always searching, always looking ahead. The problem can come, though, when one has worked out a new sermon outline, a challenging outline for both preacher and parishioners, but the outline engages the preacher's older, or past, ideas and emotions in such a way as to make memorizing the new material more difficult than it would otherwise be.

We could call this the palimpsest syndrome, a palimpsest being something that has been written on repeatedly over time, but never erased very well before something else is written on it. The traces of the old writing are always showing through, making the reading of the new somewhat difficult. It is the same thing here. It is also why one should be glad that what one learns for weekly sermon outlines is truly short-term. The erasing is important in order for the next memory process to work most efficiently. The bottom line is that when the preacher becomes aware of difficulty in memorizing a particular sequence or set of sequences, he or she should look for the interference of past ideas or buried emotional marks that might be interfering. Knowing that they could be there, or even perhaps finding them, is often a way to clear the mental air so that one's work of memorization can proceed.

There is a third element, too, that can sometimes cause interference in the memorizing process, and while it is more subtle, it can be the most common barrier that one encounters. It is an implicit glitch in the logic of the outline that one is trying to memorize. On the surface, the outline, which has been carefully crafted and evaluated, appears to move from sequence to sequence with clarity and logic. But at a deeper, subconscious level in the mind of the preacher, something is out of place, something is not quite right. Where the mind is trying to capitalize on an underlying order, it is, at the same time, saying that something is out of order; hence, the mind's memory apparatus is gently and even subtly resisting accepting it.

Even though we will talk later about what to do when one

forgets something during the preaching of the sermon, this is most often where the problem lies. One is preaching and midway through reaches for a particular sequence but cannot find it; one has forgotten what the next sequence is in what is otherwise a well-learned sermon. Usually, this means that the mind was not able to make a logical connection to the piece that is lost. The best thing to do in that case is to continue preaching and skip that sequence and go to the next one, one that is usually quite available in one's memory. Almost always, in retrospect, the preacher understands that the loss of that sequence made the overall sermon better than it was planned to be. The sequence was probably out of place, an intrusion into an otherwise logical lineup of sequences. The point is that sometimes one makes this discovery during the memorizing process, rather than when the sermon is actually preached—something for which the preacher will learn to be grateful. When one does have difficulty remembering a sequence at the memorizing stage, one should always reevaluate the sequence's place in the overall outline.

Developing Confidence in Memory

So far I have held back one of the most important dimensions of this memorizing process for preaching. It is a dimension, though, that is not so much a step as what ultimately results from learning to carry out the process itself. It has to do with a preacher's confidence in his or her mental capacities—the capacity to remember and, in a live setting, to recall what one has memorized. This is always the most surprising element for the preacher who decides to try preaching without notes—the surprising discovery that, if one has followed the established procedures, one's memory does not fail. Interferences can occur. I have emphasized that. But with some experience, one learns to recognize what those interferences are and handle them when they happen. One's memory is invariably good, and one quickly learns that it is a dependable ability. Our minds are a lot better than we have usually been taught that they are, and our capacities for memory are a lot larger and surer than we have ever really tested.

In many ways, this is the key to beginning what can be a life-time of preaching sermons every week—strong, well-prepared, challenging sermons powerfully preached without notes. Those who preach with notes believe that they cannot do without them. Those who *do* believe, and believe more intensely over the years, that they can preach without notes actually can. And with that confidence always comes a growing ease in carrying it out. Sometimes it takes only trying it once or twice. One senses early on that what others said could be done, in fact can be. The difference in congregational response to one's trying it can sometimes be quite overwhelming.

It is time, then, to turn to the memorizing process for the sermon outline and materials prepared for John Mark. There are three steps here: One is, in a sense, preliminary; the other two are of a very specific and intense nature. I have decided to devote two blocks of time, an hour each, to concentrated memorization: one Thursday afternoon and the other Friday morning. Then I will have a refresher hour on Saturday morning with a brief review Sunday morning before I preach the sermon. I will not divide the material to be memorized into two parts—I have learned that that is not the most efficient way for me. Instead, I will go through the entire repetition process during each of my two hour-long memorization periods.

The first quarter of my first hour is, in a sense, preliminary. I use it to get in my mind an overview of the sequences; it is what memory experts call the "schema," or overall pattern of the whole. I have already suggested what that is, but I will review it quickly. It begins with my opening sequence, now *28 Up,* and then has the five sequences that provide the whole of the Mark story, ending up with my first statement of the sermon's metaphor—John Mark comes back from early rejection by Paul to write a Gospel of Jesus Christ. Then, to a single sequence of my friend Jennie, whose life, in a number of ways, reflects the experience of Mark. Then, the transition to the three sequences of the sermon's conclusion: How do we still come back to write gospels in our lives, and in our times and places? There are three short, parallel sequences here. Now I have a clear sense of the overview: the opening sequence, the Mark story broken into five pieces, to Jennie, then to the three "How?" sequences with which I will wrap up.

Now I am ready to memorize the sequences themselves. Since I have repeated the overview several times, I will focus on two things primarily: first, on the sequences, and, second, on the supporting materials for Mark's life: those are the key pieces now as far as my memorizing is concerned. They include not only my specific textual notes, but also the wordings of some of the texts that I also want to use—in a specific way—in the sermon that I will preach. All of this will be done from memory. Since I have already worked carefully on these various texts, this is not nearly as difficult at this stage at it first appears to be. So:

Sequence 2—John Mark's boyhood: What do we know?

> * Acts 12:12—specifically, that he lived in Jerusalem with his mother, whose name was Mary. Story is that Peter was in prison, was released by an angel in the middle of the night, was led by the angel to the house of Mary—mother of John, also called Mark—"where many had gathered and were praying." Says a lot about Mark's growing up, though we are not told Mark was there when all of this happened. Acts written much later, and Mark was already known. But this places Mark's background. He might have been a teenager, let's say, though clearly we are guessing.

> * Mark 14:51—I will learn the verse: young man, wearing nothing but a linen garment was in the garden when Jesus was arrested. When the young man was seized, the text says, he escaped, fleeing naked into the night, leaving his garment behind. Mark? Nobody knows, but it is an odd note in the middle of an otherwise fairly straightforward story. May have been.

In each of my two memorization hours, I will go through these brief paragraphs until I know their details well, which will not take very long. I will focus intensely on the *precise* location of the Scripture verses, since I do not want to speak generally but specifically. No small amount of credibility rests on that. Here is the next sequence, then, with its supporting materials.

Sequence 3—John Mark as a young adult: Trust and Desertion

> * Acts 12:25—only a few verses after the note about Mark in 12:12. Background: Barnabas had found and befriended Saul after his conversion in Antioch. Barnabas was trusted and was selected to carry an offering from Antioch to the church in Jerusalem, which was on hard times. Barnabas took Saul with him so Barnabas could vouch for him and introduce him to the apostles there. It was a daring thing for Barnabas to do. When Barnabas and Saul have finished their mission, they return to Antioch and "brought with them John, whose other name was Mark."

> * Acts 13:4, 5—Then, only a few verses later, Barnabas and Saul are commissioned for a journey on behalf of the church (the first missionary journey), and they sail for Cyprus— Barnabas was from Cyprus—taking with them John Mark, as their helper or assistant, literally, in Greek, a rowing term suggesting "a member of the crew."

> * Acts 13:13—They leave Cyprus and sail for the mainland. Their first stop is Perga in Pamphylia, on the coast. There, as they begin their work, "John, however, left them and returned to Jerusalem." No other comment. Even the Greek term for "left" is fairly nondescript. Barnabas and Saul go on.

Sequence number 4 is a little different in the notes I have taken, since I am fascinated by some aspects of the text's language. I believe that the full drama of the story, as I want to tell it, is accented if the language (again) is allowed to convey its full weight; I will convey the drama by talking about the words themselves. Here are my notes on the sequence:

Sequence 4—The breakup of Barnabas and Paul over John Mark

* Acts 15, very end of chapter. A second journey is proposed to revisit the churches they began. Barnabas says that Mark wants to go again.

* Acts 15:38—Paul does not think it wise to take John Mark, since he "deserted" them early on first trip. "Deserted" translates a very strong Greek word that has two aspects to it: (1) It suggests a revolt or something close to that, indicating that there may have been more of a problem with Mark's earlier leaving than the text indicated at that point. And (2) it suggests a cutting off of all contact, regardless of how it happened.

* Acts 15:39—Barnabas seems to have been committed to taking Mark, and what is called in Greek a "sharp contention" flared between Barnabas and Paul. The Greek word, too, is very strong. It means a flashing of anger—an anger so strong that Paul and Barnabas parted company. Barnabas took Mark and went to Cyprus, and from then we know nothing at all. Paul picked a new companion, Silas, and was accompanied at least part of the time by Luke. We follow Paul's story from that point on. Mark disappears.

* Note: 1 Cor. 13:5—Paul's famous love chapter. The word that Paul uses in that chapter—there translated, "It [love] does not insist on its own way; it is not irritable or resentful" is the same Greek word used in Acts to describe the "sharp contention" between Paul and Barnabas.

This is the way that I have constructed my extended working outline—with the designation of a sequence and, for those sequences that call for it, a substantive written description of what I must learn for the sermon. The learning is not difficult, however, and I will repeat the details, as I have put them down here, until I know them and can tell them. Remember that I want the *specific* verses of text at each point, so I take pains to make sure I know what information is in Acts 12:12, 25; 13:5, 13 and so on. I will sketch briefly my notes under sequences five and six, since they will be somewhat different, containing my speculations and ruminations, which I consider in a sermon like this to be both legitimate and fun.

Sequence 5—Paul and John Mark back together, but how?

* Long time passes. How much? Hard to say. But we can speculate. Clue comes in finding John Mark mentioned in two letters written by Paul.

* Col. 4:10—"Aristarchus my fellow prisoner greets you, as does Mark the cousin of Barnabas." And, very important, "you have received instructions—if he comes to you, welcome him." What instructions? Whatever you have heard about him, he is OK now. Receive him.

* Philem. 24—written probably at same time from Paul's prison; the letter carried by Onesimus to Philemon: "Epaphras . . . sends greetings to you, and so do Mark. . . ."

* If Colossians was written, say, in 60 or perhaps even later, then about ten to fourteen years have passed. It's a long time. What happened in that time? Did Paul realize he had made a mistake? Did Paul have regrets? Did John Mark write to Paul? Something happened. But what? We have no idea.

* In 2 Tim. 4:11, one other important text, whether Paul wrote it or not; another might have heard Paul say it before his death. "Get Mark and bring him with you, for he is useful in my ministry." What a tribute late in Paul's life.

Sequence 6—Tragedy, and John Mark steps up to write a Gospel

* Paul is martyred in about 65 under Nero.

* By the late 60s Rome is marching on Palestine, and the destruction of Jerusalem, and with it the Jewish Temple, looms. The year 70 marks the downfall. Jews and Christians have scattered in all directions. What will happen to the story of Jesus? Records will be destroyed; notes, stories, and legends could be

lost. Paul's letters still exist here and there, at least some of them. Someone, though, must pull things together. John Mark has seen it all; he knew Peter and the others; and he had access to Paul's letters and his theology. John Mark sits down with a table full of materials, and as the world of Jerusalem and Palestine is crumbling, he writes a short story, a brilliant short story of Jesus, telling what he can remember, constructing as he must, bracing it all with Paul's christological theology. Out of it, the Christian Gospels will emerge. John Mark rose to the occasion. And the world, after that, was never the same.

By no means will I write out notes like this for every sequence, since it is not necessary. In my first sequence, the one from *28 Up,* I have two notes: one that the film was released in 1963, and the other that it was made by a young documentary filmmaker named Michael Apted. The film has won numerous awards over the years in Britain, including the British equivalent of the Academy Award. I do not need any particular notes on my Jennie sequence, since I know her story and can tell it very well, even within the context of this sermon. I have reviewed it in my head, but no memorization about it is required. Nor will I make any notes for the last three sequences. I have a clear view of what I wish to say in those sequences, and, aside from knowing the sequence titles, there is nothing specific to memorize.

Moreover, none of what I have sketched as the supporting materials under my Mark sequences is difficult to memorize. I am easily able to do it in the two one-hour sessions I have allotted. I follow the same procedure in each of the two hours I have set aside. That is, I go through the sequence titles in order, repetitiously speaking them aloud, continuing down the lis. I do it over and over again until I can almost do it without thinking about them. After twenty or twenty-five minutes of doing that, I isolate the sequences that require memorizing the supporting materials, obviously working mostly on the five Mark sequences. I take them one at a time, this time with my notes in hand, and talk aloud through them. After a half hour or so, the story—built around the order and titles of the sequences—begins to be etched in my mind.

The point here is that despite the details that must be learned, it works. I know the whole thing fairly well after that first hour. I repeat the process in exactly the same way during the second hour the next day. By the end of that second hour, I know the sermon's outline, including all of its details, by heart. On Saturday, I will go through it again a few times, but only to sharpen it up. After a refresher early Sunday I am ready to preach the sermon.

In addition, during these memorization periods, I have finally decided on the title for my sermon. Maybe it could be better, but for me, it meets the criteria that I think are important. It speaks of the heart of the sermon, yet it is also vaguely mysterious, with a "What could that mean?" quality about it. I think it keeps the sermon card turned down on the table. It also pokes at everybody a bit, maybe even a bit uncomfortably. Besides, I like it. I will call the sermon, "Writing Your Own Gospel."

Chapter Four

Delivering the Sermon Without Notes: Sunday

It is Sunday morning and we are nearing the time for delivering the sermon. It is, we think, well-prepared, but not finished. That will happen only in its delivery and its aftermath. What do we want to achieve in those moments when we are actually preaching, or speaking, our sermon? Apart from what we might say theologically, what, as public speakers, do we want to achieve? We made some suggestions in the introduction to this book, but we need to review briefly before we pull everything together and stand before the people.

It is fair to say that we want to achieve two fundamental, even indispensable, things, both related and both intricately connected to our vocation as Christian pastors, ministers, and preachers. First, we want to achieve credibility or believability. We know from years of research in public speech and communication that what is called source credibility is the basis of message credibility. We think "I will believe what you say if I have developed a sense that you are believable." We know other things as well. For example, we know that source credibility is not so much about the nature of the source as it is about the public's *perception* of that source. Often, the two things can be correlated, but frequently they are not. It is not uncommon for a message to be both timely and important, even urgent, and yet it is not believed since the source of the message did not come across as credible. We also know that source credibility is built, at one level, from the background of the speaker, but, at a far greater level, it is built from how the message is actually delivered. What we see and hear greatly affects what we believe.

In addition to credibility, though, we also want in our sermon delivery to achieve a maximum level of intimacy. This is tricky in public address, because it means that even though we speak to a large number of people at once, we want every individual to feel personally talked to. That is what intimacy in public speaking means. We want everyone to go away thinking that what the preacher said "had me in mind." We want those words "You spoke to me today" to be the aftermath of the sermon we have preached. It is this kind of direct involvement with the sermon that we hope everyone who shares the sermon will experience. We want people to get caught up in the preaching. It is possible to speak to several hundred people or more at once and still achieve that kind of intimate involvement.

I now turn to the specific issues of effectively delivering the sermon preached without notes. One matter must be dealt with before we get to the details of public address: Where should the preacher without notes stand? Sometimes this is not a question, since the preacher has no choice. The pulpit is situated so that the preacher must, regardless of how he or she delivers the sermon, stand behind it, and even occasionally be bound within its walled construction. I should emphasize that even if the preacher is confined within or behind a pulpit, preaching without notes is *always* more effective than having manuscript or notes present on the pulpit. It is simply not true that being lodged within or behind a large pulpit means that congregants cannot tell whether or not one has a manuscript or notes. Congregants can tell because the preacher standing behind the pulpit speaking without notes gives the sermon life and energy, credibility and intimacy that it does not otherwise have. The congregation knows; preachers should not fool themselves.

Whether one uses a pulpit or not, to preach without notes is to rise to a higher level of credibility and intimacy with a congregation than one can achieve when pages or cards are in front of one's eyes.

It is increasingly understood, though, that standing out of the pulpit, on an open platform of some kind at the front of the chancel, or in some other appropriate open space, provides the most effective setting for the delivery of the sermon without notes. Here one stands holding only a small Bible, if anything at all. Being empty-handed is preferable to holding anything, since the hands are needed for effective gesturing. Nothing at all need stand between the preacher and the congregants. Moreover, the preacher, whether dressed in street clothes or clerical robe, is seen from head to foot by the congregants. One of the basic principles of human interaction is that the more of a speaker's body that is visible, the more he or she is able to hold the audience's attention. If one can comfortably stand away from the pulpit to deliver the sermon, one should do so. Sometimes, when the preacher first moves from pulpit to platform, a congregation not used to the change of position may balk a bit. My experience, confirmed by many others, is that after a couple of weeks of experiencing such sermons, the congregation is grateful for the new directness between preacher and people that comes with the more open position.

I am aware that suggesting that women pastors should stand outside of the pulpit when possible can be problematic when they are not wearing a robe or clerical gown. The issue of appropriate dress is one that each individual must work through either on her own or in consultation with other women clergy. However, my experience is that when women who preach are elegantly and conservatively attired—as male clergy without gown should also be—their presence outside of the pulpit, speaking directly and without notes, is both engaging and energizing, whatever the speaking style.

The Elements of Effective Speaking

So what difference does it make in our public speaking, our preaching, when we preach without notes? I can best answer this basic question by reviewing some of the fundamental elements of good public speaking, elements that one can find spelled out in detail in any college speech textbook. After I have done that, I will conclude with a listing of twelve specific directions for working at maximum effectiveness, without notes, in the pulpit.

Public speaking involves two large dimensions—what are usually called its nonverbal dimension and its more obvious verbal one. How well the preacher understands and deals with both of these dimensions literally determines the degree to which he or she is able to achieve both credibility and intimacy in the delivery of the sermon. Both of these are *always* in play whenever anyone stands up to speak.

Five elements make up the nonverbal, or the physical behavioral, dimension of the speaking process—elements that every preacher not only learns to practice, but should diligently polish and sharpen over the years.

1. *Good Posture.* One of the great benefits of preaching without notes is that it lowers the sense of rigidity, if not formality, in preaching. Everyone is more at ease, something that both preacher and congregants appreciate. This makes the call to good posture a particularly important one. Despite the informality that the preacher may experience, he or she still must—in either pulpit or on open platform—stand fully erect, alert, poised, and balanced. There are rules here, among them that there shall be no leaning on the pulpit if one should stand beside it. There shall be no rocking from side to side in any kind of regular motion, no shifting from one foot to the other. It is possible to stand erect and poised, and at the same time to be relaxed and comfortable. Men should never stand with their hands in their jacket pockets or pants pockets, which is always a serious temptation when one is not holding onto

notes or books. One should not play with jewelry or change, whether in one's pockets or not. One should not button and unbutton one's jacket. One should not hold tightly to the hanging ends of one's stole. One's whole posture is crucial to how congregants perceive the preacher during the sermon. Relaxed dignity is what most look for, and this is conveyed, in large part, by how one stands as one delivers the sermon.

2. *Movement.* While maintaining good posture always, the preacher working without notes should feel free to move around—not to the point of wearying the congregants, which can be done, but as a way of both holding attention and sustaining interest. Further, the rule is that one should make no unpurposeful or irrelevant movements. That is, one does not move for the sake of moving. One moves in harmony with what one is saying. Movement is also, at times, a form of relief in the sermon. It is a way to let people breathe, to shift in their seats. It also allows both preacher and people alike to change rhythms, to shift emotionally and cathartically, just as the preacher moves physically.

One does not plan one's moves—in fact, one should never try to do so—even though it is important to have a clear sense of where and how one *can* move comfortably. That is, the preacher should become very familiar with the range and nature of the space available for any movements. In the pulpit, of course, such movements are minimized, and other forms of motion, such as gestures (which I shall discuss later), will become particularly useful. Sometimes, one may choose to begin the sermon in the pulpit and at some point move out of it and even back into it, but this should never be done in a way that calls undue attention to itself, nor should one develop a habit of walking back and forth from pulpit to platform.

I am talking about two types of body movements. The first is simply walking: steps taken at appropriate points to one side or the other, or forward and back. Sometimes one may walk down a step or two to another level, or simply stand on a step. One learns quickly, though, that one must be able to see such steps well, particularly over bifocals; the last thing one wants to do is miss a step. The second type of body movement is of a dramatic nature. One may act something out and utilize a kind of controlled pantomime in order to do it. One may talk about a form of surprise that causes one to jump back. In this sense, the preacher can treat the platform as a stage, which it is. This can all be overdone, of course; but when it is done boldly and yet under control, it brings to the sermon life and vitality that can be achieved in no other way.

One of my students in an advanced preaching class was a professional actor for some twenty years before deciding to enter seminary and ministry. His first preaching experiences amounted to a kind of anti-acting. No movement whatsoever, and even few gestures. He knew well what he wanted to say, even though he had to be coaxed, first, to give up his notes, which he did. It took even more coaxing before he began blending his preaching skills with his acting skills. As he gained a sense of how to do this, he preached a sermon about Zacchaeus in a Claremont chapel service in which he worked from the center platform in front of the chancel. He, too, is short, so he used his stature as part of his sermon on Zacchaeus, making it both fun and insightful. He pantomimed the story with a remarkably restrained vigor, having Zacchaeus climb the tree, work hard to position himself on a limb that was already loaded with kids who had also climbed the tree, and then hurry to get down when singled out by Jesus. It was an unforgettable sermon, filled with movement, energy, and great fun.

3. *Eye Contact.* Everyone knows eye contact is important, but not everyone realizes that research has demonstrated a direct ratio between the effectiveness of eye contact and the effectiveness of what is being said. What audience research has plainly taught us, in fact, is that one of the most significant ingredients in high credibility accorded to a public speaker is the consistency and intensity of the speaker's eye contact. And nothing serves eye contact better than learning to preach without notes.

Reading a manuscript in the pulpit, of course, virtually curtails any sustained eye contact, no matter how effectively one can read aloud. With notes, the preacher is able to maintain some eye contact, but surprisingly little, since keeping track of one's notes requires a significant amount of looking down. One of the major reasons why the very best public speakers use no notes is because they want that eye contact with those to whom they speak to be virtually unbroken. The eye contact is the bond between speaker—in this case the preacher—and the congregants. Good eye contact does not mean that one focuses on one or two or a half dozen people in the congregation. It means that one takes in literally the entire congregation with one's eyes. Every person gets looked at, focused on. The speaker's eyes move, landing momentarily on eyes here and there and over there. The speaker's eyes sweep slowly across the entire group, regardless of its size; then they sweep back and again. With changes in this sweeping pattern, the eye movement does its bonding work. If there are people in a balcony, the eye movement does the same there. Even if there is a choir to one side, or at one's back, one who preaches without notes can easily move in such a way as to establish eye contact in every direction in which there are people. The appreciation for that kind of intense, wide-ranging eye contact will be unending. This kind of powerful eye contact is only possible without notes.

A good speaker may look away from the people for a fleeting moment now and then, mostly to break tension or to engage a thought, neither of which actually breaks audience contact. Unlike looking down at one's notes, which for a time turns loose of the audience, or congregants, looking away in order to provide a kind of release does not allow the audience to go away. On the contrary, it can have the opposite effect, compelling the audience to stay more intently fixed on the speaker.

4. *Gestures.* Gestures are body movements, but, more specifically, movements of the head and shoulders, hands and arms. However, many of the things that we said about larger body

movements may be said here as well. Gestures must not be forced or artificial in any way. They must always be integrally related to, and arise from, what is being said. They must match what is being said, when it is being said. Gestures, in this sense, must be natural. They must also be dynamic, which means that they are to accent the movement and flow of the voice. They emerge from what is said, not in any planned or scripted way, not even in a coached way. We can see this by the ways in which we actually carry on conversations with each other, the ways we speak to each other normally, naturally. Every such conversation is accentuated with, and aided by, natural, spontaneous gestures. Our hands, arms, shoulders, and head all play key roles in our talking; some would say that we cannot talk to each other without all of these parts coming into play. It is true. But it is just as true for one who would be a truly effective public speaker.

Manuscripts and notes in the pulpit are a severe detriment to the use of gestures when one speaks in front of people. Gestures, when they actually are used, tend to be both limited and awkward. Most of the time they seem contrived. When a manuscript is read, spontaneity is lost, and with that the power of gestures is lost as well. When notes are used, one's hands and arms tend to hover around the note pages or cards. One must move the pieces around, and do so at the right times, so one's attention is divided between that and trying to let gestures involving the hands and arms emerge as they can. Gestures, including eye contact, can only work their full magic in public speaking when one preaches without notes. The emphasis here is on the word "allowed." It is true that one can, at first, be very self-conscious about one's hands, not knowing what to do with them or where to put them. It is only with practice that one learns how to become natural with one's hands and gestures. When no gestures are called for, it's often best to let one's arms rest at one's sides. Sometimes folding one's hands together at the waist is a good resting position, as long as one does not engage in nervous movement of some kind. Gestures should come into play when one is saying something that calls for them. One will, with experience, know when and how to make that happen. One can even become very animated with one's gestures, making one's presence come alive not only with sound, but also with matching movements. The power of it all can be electrifying when one learns to do it well.

5. *Facial Expression.* Again, voluminous speech research over the course of the twentieth century has more than demonstrated that a speaker's own attitude—the attitude to which audience or congregants respond most intensely—is conveyed by a speaker's face. There are often subtleties here, but seldom any deep ambiguities. People know how to read faces; they know faces that are interested, happy, amused, cynical, troubled, or sad. Our moods are in our faces. We may try to hide our moods in many ways, but our faces invariably give us away.

We tend to watch a speaker's face looking for two things. We look for the degree to which the face matches the words that are being spoken. Is this a sad preacher speaking happy words? Why? Which, then, should we believe? Does the face convey cynicism while the words being spoken are supposed to be reassuring? What we somehow know is that when confronted with some face/word dichotomy, we are best advised to believe the face instead of the words. This is a problem with preachers and preaching. We think our sermons are in our words, so we try to get them said as expeditiously as we can. Yet, from the viewpoint of those who listen to us, our sermons are, at a deeper level, in our faces, and we would do well to know that our facial expressions and our words had best match.

The second thing we look for in facial expression is the level, or, better, the depth, of interest in what is being said in the words of the sermon. Again, it seems to be a human trait that we can read other people's faces in this way. We can always tell when someone is really interested in, or involved in, what he or she is saying. Often we can tell it in the nature of the speaking itself, as we shall see momentarily, but we can always tell it in the excited shifts and turns of the speaker's facial expressions. A speaker's interested face tends to be vibrant and animated. No facial expression is planned. Subtleties of language, idea, argument, and story are reflected directly in shifts in look and expression—from wide-eyed to searching to frowning slightly to a wrinkled, questioning forehead. People, congregants, read it all. They measure credibility in our facial movements. Moreover, as we suggested earlier, congregants tend to become as interested and involved in what those facial expressions show as the one who creates those expressions.

Verbal Meaning in the Pulpit

This takes us through the nonverbal dimensions of public speaking. There are also verbal ones, though in many ways they are not as complex or even as significant as the nonverbal ones. The verbal ones, of course, concern the use of one's voice. The verbal and the nonverbal go together, or at least in effective speaking they do. Emphases are made not with one or the other, but with both in harmony, both spontaneously working together.

One "plays" one's voice in public speaking, and particularly in preaching. The use of the voice also involves five dimensions, though we need not spend nearly as much time on them as we did on the nonverbal dimensions. They simply are not as complicated as the nonverbal are. The first of these dimensions is the voice's pitch, which is its rising and falling. Here, preachers must be warned against falling into any predictable pitch patterns. When pattern emerges, a certain monotony sets in, particularly when people must listen to the same speaker over and over again. Repetitive pitch patterns tend to take over a public address, and what is actually being said with words can get lost once the listener becomes conscious of the pattern.

Unfortunately, falling into a set pitch pattern is often what happens when one reads one's own speeches, or sermons, from a manuscript week in and week out. When one speaks without notes and one's words come with a high degree of spontaneity, it is very difficult for pitch patterns to emerge, and when they do, the speaker often becomes aware of them quickly, usually without others' coaching. One's pitch reflects great variety and lively movements as the voice becomes as fully animated as one's face, hands, and body. What one wants, and what preaching without notes allows, is a natural elasticity to guide the range of one's pitch. The shifts in pitch, in this sense, are natural, as they should be.

Other dimensions of voice are range, volume, and speed; all ways of forming emphasis vocally, verbally. One raises one's voice, we say, either in its range or in its volume, for emphasis or to create a particular impression. One can also do the same things by lowering one's voice, by dropping its register or its volume. There is also the rate at which one speaks, meaning the speeding up or the slowing down of one's speech. We can talk fast as a way to emphasize something, or we can slow down, not just to deemphasize, but also to create other kinds of impressions as well.

Finally, there is what speech teachers call voice quality, which is a way to talk about the unique characteristics of one's voice. No two voices, as we know well, are ever alike; we can now produce voiceprints that are the verbal equivalents of fingerprints. We can be identified by our voiceprints. We each have unique voices and in public speaking we should never try to sound like someone else. It never works. It always creates a cloying artificiality. Every voice has its own identity, and every voice is, in its own way, pleasant and listenable. Cultivating one's own voice, with its own distinctive qualities, is one of the most important things that the preacher can do. When the preacher does that, consciously and over time, then the voice and the personality match. The preacher in the pulpit, or on the platform, is all of one piece. Once a preacher knows that, he or she has laid the basis for the fullest possible credibility and intimacy in the sermon experience.

Having said all that, then, it is time not just to summarize, but also to bring everything to a focus in the remarkable moments of preaching without notes. What follow are twelve things to remember in order to be at your very best when you stand before people to deliver your sermon.

Twelve Ways to Sharpen the Sermon Without Notes

1. Plan to be nervous in the hours and minutes before you preach. For some preachers, this potential nervousness is reason enough for finishing the sermon manuscript on Friday afternoon, reviewing and even reworking it a bit on Sunday morning, and then reading it from the pulpit. But the fact is that many manuscript preachers also get nervous as the time for the sermon nears. Planning to preach without notes, however, is to raise the level of nervousness to heights that manuscript preachers will probably never know. Nervousness before one preaches a sermon without notes is as expected—and normal—as it is for the most seasoned professional stage actor. In fact, some years ago the television program *60 Minutes* featured a segment on one of the twentieth century's greatest actors, Laurence Olivier. He had won every accolade that the world's stages had to give, but he confessed to perpetual stage fright, a sense of terror before every performance. He had learned over the years to recognize and cope with it, but not to eliminate it.

Before the sermon, there is the buildup within the preacher, the flow of adrenalin. There is the sense of "Can I do this?" "Of course I can do this." Most speech scholars describe this as a kind of anxiety, but a very healthy anxiety, and one that evaporates as soon as one actually begins to speak. But the buildup of anxiety, or stage fright, is precisely what raises the occasion to the peak of its potential. Everything is held back, like pulling a rubber band taut, until the moment of speaking, when the tension of holding back is released with enormous energy and power once the sermon is finally preached. The experience, under such circumstances, is always profoundly memorable, as almost anyone can describe from some personal experience.

Recognizing this means that in the few hours on Sunday morning before the sermon, the preacher will minimize other activities, will set in motion the focusing process, will let the building process, with all of its tension, begin naturally. It means that in the half hour or so before the service, the preacher will find a quiet place to be alone. The study door will be closed and locked, and he or she will concentrate on bringing the preaching experience fully into view. This is not the time to go over one's outline one last time—it is too late for that—but to let one's spirit and God's spirit prepare for releasing what one has prepared to say. It will be, in that sense, a time for prayer, but more than that, it is a time for concentrated meditation and shutting out everything else and focusing on the sermon.

2. Speak naturally and conversationally. Too many preachers still try to conjure up a voice for preaching, a voice that is different from the one with which they usually talk, and even different from the one with which they will greet people at the end of the worship service. To preach without notes, though, is just to talk. It is to carry on a conversation, in public, with a group of one's friends who have come to share a particular time and place. Even in church, people want to be talked to, not preached at. Talking, in this sense, is preaching, and preaching is talking. The conversation, on its surface, is one-sided, with the preacher doing all of the talking. Yet, in a real sense, it is not one-sided at all if the preacher actually engages the congregation. When that happens, every head in the sanctuary is alive with silent responding, ruminating, thinking through, arguing with everything that the preacher is saying at the very moment the preacher is saying it. Some of these internal conversations will probably be picked up later, audibly, in various settings; some may even include the preacher.

This natural speech, this conversational preaching, must be

highly animated, of course. We have already talked about that. It is not dull or quiet as it comes from the preacher. It is not delivered deadpan. By the same token, the most interesting and lively conversations we have in one-on-one situations or small-group settings are not dull and quiet, and certainly not delivered deadpan. They are alive, filled with all of the movements, gestures, attentive eyes, and animated faces about which I spoke earlier. The preacher in natural speech does raise his or her voice, does hem and haw occasionally, does break sentences off in order to start new ones, does catch something that was said and try to redo it as the speaking itself proceeds. This is normal speech. It is also normal, and highly effective, public speaking.

3. The preacher should not try to hide or disguise his or her emotions during the delivery of the sermon. At the very heart of preaching without notes is the freeing of one's emotions. This is what we mean when we talk about hearing a sermon that was preached from the heart. It was filled with ideas, with theology, with good thoughts, but what really undergirded the entire sermon was a firm and visible emotional base. The preacher really felt this. The sermon touched me, people in the congregation will say, which is another way of saying that the preacher touched me. Human connections are made, we know, when two or more people truly open up, saying what they genuinely feel; that is langauge we all use. It brings home to us that the connections we make most powerfully and lastingly with each other are *emotional* connections. Such connections happen when our emotions are allowed to rise to the surface, are allowed to become visible through all of the ways we have of revealing ourselves to each other.

We know very well now that the greatest sermons are invariably emotionally based. They tend to be preached best at crisis moments in our individual and collective lives. But knowing that only presents us with the tip of the iceberg. Within us all, constantly, are reservoirs of emotion and feeling, those ingredients that give rise to our speaking about the things most profoundly important to us; that, too, is what makes for great preaching. I am not talking about outpourings of tears in the pulpit. In fact, it is questionable whether tears have any place in the pulpit at all, since, at least in our time, they create more embarrassment for congregants than anything else. Nor am I talking about a preacher ranting and raving, mopping up sweat with a handkerchief as the sermon proceeds. Not at all. I am talking about a sense of control and even appropriateness as one speaks to people. But even while staying in control and using appropriate forms of behavior, pastors can express the full range of emotions. We can be passionate. We can say what we are really thinking and feeling. We can, if you please, occasionally pound the pulpit, even if metaphorically.

4. Try to never think ahead. Let the preparation of your sermon carry you along at its own speed. This is one of the more common mistakes made when learning to preach without notes. One tries to remember what is coming up later at the same time that one is speaking. A good speaker knows, though, that one is asking for trouble the minute that one thinks ahead. It tends to confuse what one is saying at that moment, and, more important, it tends to confuse what one was *going* to say later when one gets to it.

Not thinking ahead of oneself is achieved through a full and complete trust in one's own memory. Most preachers who begin to preach without notes are amazed at how well their memories actually work. Their abilities to remember are far superior to what they have even imagined before they used them in this way. When the sermon begins, though, the preacher must kick the memory process into automatic. No second guessing it now. No trying to go over the sermon's ending in the back of the mind while the front of the mind is preaching the opening sequences. It will not work. A person must trust the memory to do its thing. For the most part, it may falter occasionally, but it will not fail. It will carry one through. One must have the discipline to follow it where and how it leads.

5. If you do forget something at the moment you need it, go on to where your memory takes you. No one but you, the preacher, will know you have missed something. No one but you *should* know. The important thing is that one not react in any visible or overt way to having forgotten. Pick up at your next sequence as though you had planned it that very way. Actually forgetting a sequence when one comes to it is something that happens only rarely. I have already suggested that, when you look back later, you may very well discover that the sequences are even better if your mind chooses to drop one out. But the important thing is: Do not panic or do anything to tip off the congregation that something has gone awry. There is no need for histrionics when this happens, no need to announce that one has forgotten something, no need to squeeze one's face up, creating what would surely become a few moments of unnecessary awkwardness. One takes one's normal break between sequences, or where transitions have been planned, picks up where one's memory dictates, and then goes on as though nothing unusual has happened.

6. View the overall sermon, whatever it is and whatever it is about, as a drama. View the delivery of your sermon as the telling of a wonderful story that you have devised, one filled with verve and passion, with an exciting ending that cannot be known until the end. This means that one should view the sermon as starting at one level, a friendly low level, we might say, and then building in intensity and excitement, each piece adding another dimension to the story that one is spinning. Some parts of the story are theological, and carefully selected for what they will add to this particular story. The sermon can create suspense and tension as it moves along, building toward where you are taking it. Early in the sermon, congregants should wonder where this is going, and even halfway or more through be able to say to themselves "I know this is headed someplace, I can sense that, but I don't see the destination yet."

This brings us back to the inductive sermon. Regardless of how one conceives of it, it is a sermon form ideally suited to be preached without notes. One should preach inductively, without notes, and then take full advantage of the convergence of two remarkable processes, an inductively prepared sermon and an inductively delivered sermon. One can create a fine and captivating sense of drama, of dramatic progression and outcome, not only by letting the sermon unfold inductively, but also by using all of the tools of the preacher's own dramatic presence and voice to contribute to the telling of the story. What we earlier called the sequences of our sermon outline become, in some ways, the acts in the drama or the play, which is the sermon. Each act, in this sense, carries the play, the sermon, to a slightly higher level, and in our preaching without notes, we are able to give full realization to this experience of the sermon.

7. Every now and then, in the sermon preached without notes, the preacher does feel compelled to read something as part of the sermon. This should not become a habit, and, in fact, should only be done when the piece is so unique and so compelling on its own that telling it or telling about it will not do. When it happens, the preacher should set up the reading, should tell the congregants that he or she wishes to share something special—"I want to read something very unusual to you"—and proceed to the item: a stunning quotation, a short, moving (or funny) piece from a newspaper or magazine, or part of a letter that one has received. The paper containing the quotation should be kept on the pulpit or nearby stand until it is needed, not held through the sermon. As one sets up its use in the sermon, one retrieves it, and after it has been carefully read, one returns it to the pulpit or stand where it was. The act of reading itself is treated as part of the sermon's progression. It will work well if (a) it is not done very often; and (b) if the preacher treats both the act of reading and the reading of this particular piece as an unusual event in the preaching of the sermon.

8. Interact with the congregants as you preach. This is one of the most powerful aspects of preaching without notes, real-

izing a power that can be achieved in no other way. In preaching this way, one watches the congregation as closely as one is watched by it. One *really* sees people, and even though one focuses on what one is saying, one's mind is still alive and able to register what one is seeing while speaking.

At points congregants can easily give off a message of puzzlement—sometimes a collective message of puzzlement—at something that was said. Responding to that puzzlement would not only be appropriate, but probably deeply appreciated by the congregants. One says, "You all look puzzled at what I just said; I probably didn't make myself clear. Let me try again. What I am trying to suggest to you is that...." And one works at it again. Very often, such a second attempt clarifies the source of the puzzlement, and the congregants are pleased that they had a hand in how the sermon actually unfolded. Some good manuscript preachers, too, can back off of the manuscript from time to time in response to something that they may pick up, but for most manuscript preachers those are very rare occurrences, since getting back to the manuscript often proves difficult.

One quickly learns that when preaching without notes there are a thousand usually unplanned ways in which the preacher actually responds to something that takes place within the congregational setting while the sermon is being preached. The preacher makes adjustments as he or she goes, depending on the nature of the moment or some unusual configuration of setting. The preacher may sense something that requires an adjustment of a particular sequence: It needs toning down; it needs to be kicked up. The congregants are down, and the sermon needs to be lightened somewhat in order to adjust to the congregational mood. These are real things, and the interactions between preacher and congregants are readily communicated and understood back and forth. It is the preacher's job to read what is going on both before and during the sermon. When one has memorized one's outline well and knows what one is going to say, adjustments come easily. Those adjustments usually take a very good sermon and raise it to an even higher level, as far as the congregation is concerned.

9. Be receptive to unexpected insights while preaching. While it is clearly the task of the preacher without notes to stay close to the well-prepared and memorized outline, one will discover very quickly that there are clearly times when unexpected insights occur to one while one is actually preaching. This is altogether expected, since the mind is actively thinking and even probing the materials of the sermon while verbalizing those thoughts. Often one is doing this with a keener concentration and focus than one had at any point in the preparation process. So one's best ideas can sometimes emerge out of the act of preaching itself. John Broadus commented on this years ago, saying that "any man [or woman] who possesses, even in an humble degree, the fervid oratorical nature, will find that after careful preparation, some of the noblest and most inspiring thoughts he [or she] ever gains will come while . . . engaged in speaking."[1]

What should one do when this happens? First, be aware of its happening, as one undoubtedly will be. Second, one should not be afraid to make a split-second decision as to whether or not to go with it. Sometimes it will not be the best thing to do, since one may very well sense that some dead-end road might lay at the end of an inspirational flight. On the other hand, the advice that comes from the history of those who have preached without notes is that when one is truly inspired, and that inspiration has grown out of one's careful preparation, one must go with the inspiration. Since, presumably, one preaching without notes will have followed this book's advice in thoroughly preparing the sermon, the best advice, then, is to follow the grandeur wherever a sermon's moment leads, in the full understanding that one's outline will bring one back to the trail at the appropriate moment. In truth, with experience, the preacher without notes will learn not only to value and even try to create such soaring moments, but will also develop simple and efficient ways of dealing with them in the context of well-organized sermons.

10. Have fun with the sermon. I can hear your response now, "With every sermon, even very serious ones?" The answer is yes. Can it be done? Invariably it can. This does not mean that one turns every sermon into a comedy routine, nor does it mean that every sermon should produce laughs. Even comedic sermons are not all laughter. But one of the great joys and benefits of the sermon preached without notes is that it can and should be endlessly playful. In fact, the more serious the subject or material of the sermon, the lighter and more playful should be its presentation. Every sermon should have a playfulness about it, a twinkle to it, a sense of lightness, a refusal to take itself too seriously—something that is not only easy to do, but almost natural when one preaches the sermon without notes.

The preacher is thinking out loud and just talking, and by considering it fun, it becomes fun. The preacher can speak of deep things, theological things, biblical things, but even this can all be done playfully, wryly, by pondering the folly of humanness and understanding the sense of frailty that we all bring to this experience. As one of my students put it, referring specifically to the sermon process, "The church that plays together stays together." That, in many ways, gets to the heart of it.

11. Despite the need for playfulness, one should always maintain one's dignity. Because of the nature of informality or the playfulness of preaching without notes, it is easy for the preaching situation to get out of hand. This is particularly true when one preaches regularly from a platform or open area in front of the congregation. It is easy, in other words, for everything to get a little sloppy or too cute or too interactive. When that happens, the sermon, no matter how important or well prepared, can be undermined. That, in fact, is one of the reasons that preaching without notes sometimes gets a bad reputation. One can walk around a bit when one preaches without notes—in fact, as we said earlier, doing that can be very important—but when one strides up and down an aisle or

walks out around the edges of the congregation, amplified by a lapel microphone, things have a way of coming apart. Maintain dignity—not formality or even staidness—in the midst of the animation and playfulness that preaching without notes allows.

12. Allow enough time to come down from the sermon. Finally, when the sermon that is preached without notes is over, and after the post-service formalities and greetings are finished, allow another hour or so alone to come down from the sermon. This is as important as the sense of building up to the sermon. Here, it may mean delaying lunch for a while. It may mean passing up lunch with friends immediately after church on Sunday. It may mean staying behind in the study for awhile after one's family has gone on home.

This time is not for reliving or even evaluating the sermon that one has preached. What one usually experiences during this time—particularly when one has preached without notes—is a kind of post-sermon blues. It is the letdown that comes after one has preached with great intensity and adrenalin. One is tempted to stew about what one might have said, what one left out, what one forgot that should have been said, how it might have been put together differently than it was. One can always second-guess oneself at this stage, yet one should simply acknowledge that these after-sermon feelings and thoughts are normal and expected, and then try not to second-guess what one has done. The hour or so after the service spent alone is an important time of turning loose of the sermon, a time to let the forgetting begin.

This is not to say that one cannot or should not learn from the experience each time one preaches. It is to say, though, that when one preaches a carefully prepared sermon without notes the result is almost always better, sometimes dramatically better, than one realizes in the first hours after the sermon is finished. At this stage, one should pay relatively little attention to any criticisms that anyone, including one's family members, might have; one should also pay relatively little attention to the compliments that will most likely be forthcoming. The forgetting of the sermon must begin—the sermon is mentally filed away—so that the mind begins to clear in anticipation of the sermon to be launched in earnest the next day. The transition period from one sermon to the next is that hour or two after the sermon has been preached.

In Conclusion

One other matter in conclusion. How long should the sermon preached without notes be? There is no clear answer to that question. However, when one preaches as I have proposed in this book, the length of the sermon, except in rare places or on rare occasions, becomes irrelevant. To prepare well and preach well without notes is to hold people tightly in one's hands. It is to command attention and not let go of it. Congregants are more than willing to give this attention. Time will stop for the duration of the sermon, and people will only look at their watches *after* the sermon is over. Then, more often than not, the discussion of the sermon will begin. These are the kinds of sermons that people talk about when they are over—in cars as people drive home, over lunch where a group gathers regularly after church, or even between adults and teenagers as the matters taken up in the sermon have found their ways into minds and hearts.

Appendix

Working Manuscript of a Sermon Preached Without Notes: "Writing Your Own Gospel"

Ten or so years ago, I happened to see a movie, or I thought it was going to be a movie, on public television; it turned out to be a documentary produced by the BBC in England. It was one of those rare things that you see every now and then that you know you will never forget. Its impact on me was enormous, and I have seen it in later versions since. It was called *28 Up*. But I have to describe it for you. In the early 1960s, a young British filmmaker named Michael Apted selected a group of English schoolchildren. They were from several schools, as I remember, so that they represented a cross section of kids from very different economic backgrounds. He picked a dozen or so of them, and they were all seven years old. He brought them together for what looked like a day—first of playing together, as kids do, on what appeared to be a school playground, and then he, well, interviewed them. In some cases, he interviewed only one child at a time, but in other instances, he let some who were already friends stay together, being interviewed as they sat on a sofa facing the camera. Two girls I particularly remember were together, clearly from a lower socioeconomic group; and three boys—those three boys together were unforgettable. They were from a well-to-do class, and all three already knew it.

He just interviewed them—seven-year-olds. He asked them typical questions that one would put to seven year olds: What do you want to be when you grow up? What do you think about girls—or boys, to the girls? And on to other things, like: What do you think is wrong with the world and what would you do to fix it? The answers were cute and funny, all typical kid answers. All dozen or so—I don't remember how many exactly—were interviewed that way.

What the filmmaker did, then, was put the film away for seven years. And seven years later, he went back and found those same dozen or so kids that we had met when they were seven, and Apted sat them down and interviewed them again. Now they were all fourteen, awkward, early teenagers. Most didn't want to talk. But they were there. It was remarkable to see. You could recognize them all, of course. Their views of things had changed. Now their problems were those of teenagers. Typical teenagers. What was striking in each case was thinking back on how each child had changed in seven years.

After those interviews, the filmmaker put the film away again—for another seven years. Now, when he refound his group, they were scattered, harder to find, and at least one was in prison and unavailable, as I recall. Now they were all twenty-one years old. A few were on drugs, bummed out; we had seen them when they were seven and carefree. Two, as I recall, were married, one already divorced. They were all on their own now, and life was not easy. The only ones it did appear easy for were those three well-to-do little boys who were now all in elite English schools, becoming lawyers and doctors. At twenty-one.

Then, one more time, the filmmaker put everything away— again for seven years—and, remarkably, remarkably, he managed to find most of his, well, kids again seven years later, when they were all twenty-eight. Adults now, full adults. Some making careers, others just trying to hold clerical or waitressing-types of jobs. A couple out of work. But there they were. Grown up. One, at twenty-eight, I will never forget. At seven, he had been one of the quietest, shyest of the group. At fourteen, he had been a gangly, still-very-shy teenager, but you could tell at fourteen how really bright he was. Shy but becoming quite articulate. At twenty-one, he still didn't know what he would do, but something in the sciences perhaps. At twenty-eight, the filmmaker found him, newly married, living in the United States and working on his doctor's degree in nuclear engineering at the University of Wisconsin. We knew him at age seven. Remarkable.

I should tell you that since I saw that film when everyone was twenty-eight, I have since seen a more recent version, where the group—or what was left of it—were thirty-five, where that trio of wealthy boys had indeed become barristers and prominent young members of British society, where the small, pugnacious fighter at age seven had become a London cabbie with a wife and two small children, and a take on the world that was actually articulated at age seven. And I learned recently that a new version of the film is now out, with the group back—at age forty-two. I have not seen that one.

Over the years since it was *28 Up*, the film has won numerous awards, including the British equivalent of the Academy Award. What was so remarkable about it for me when I first saw it—and still is, I guess—was that it made me deeply conscious, in a way that I have never been conscious before, of the long trajectory of a life, in this case, my life. It is one thing to make a documentary movie of an hour on the life of so-and-so, and we get a lot of those now on A&E and other places. It is something very different when one actually sees and hears how an individual, a common person, thinks and feels over long intervals of time—intervals that reveal just how we all change and yet stay the same over time.

Let me put it this way. Think back—you can do this—think back over the course of your own life. Some of you have quite a few decades behind you. We all plan to have a few more ahead of us. This will be a little harder for some of you younger folk, but play along as best you can. Let's say you had to divide your life up, not at seven-year intervals, but as decades, and let's say you are going to give a title—write a title—for each of the decades of your life. What would the title be of your teenage years—that decade from, say, age ten to twenty or twenty-one? What would it be called? Go ahead, think about that. Like, "Found the person of my dreams— planned to live happily ever after." Or, "Had ambitions to fly— I was going to be an airplane pilot and then an astronaut." Or, "We moved when I was fifteen and I lost all my friends; so for me from fifteen to twenty was miserable." Or, "Wanted to go to college—didn't get to." How would you characterize your teen decade? Sum it up?

How would you characterize you twenties? What were things like? What did you become? What did you want to become that you did not? Your thirties—what were they like? What happened that shaped that decade for you? That was the decade for me—I was thirty-three—when everything came apart. It actually was; I'm talking about myself. Everything was going good until I was thirty-three. Then I blew it. Your forties. Go on. I'm throwing it back to you. Strange to think about your life like that, isn't it? We can all look back on such things, even though no two of us will look back on our lives in the same way.

The reason I tell you about that wonderful and moving film today is to take you to a New Testament character—we have been looking in recent weeks at the lives of some little-known people of the Bible, and today I want to introduce you to one who is given to us much as the people in that film are. In a sense, we get a movie of his life, but not in a continuous form. More like *28 Up*—we meet him at various times from his youth through his adult years. And it is a remarkable and informative story.

His name is John Mark. Or just Mark. Some of you know something about him, but only a bit, of course, since we are not told very much about him at all. We get his life basically by decades, with a glimpse here and a glimpse there. But enough, over time, for us to piece his life together. It's a good story.

Let me tell you briefly what we know of John Mark. We first

meet him in the book of Acts, chapter 12, verse 12. Peter, the apostle, was in prison but was released from prison in the middle of the night by an angel. The angel led him, we are told, to a house where many people were gathered and praying, praying for Peter. It was the house of Mary, who is referred to as the mother of John, also called Mark. So, John Mark grew up in that house, and he apparently knew a lot of apostles and other Christian leaders of the time. John Mark knew Peter, and at the end of 1 Peter in our New Testament there is a reference to "my son Mark," probably John Mark. How old Mark was at this point, we can only guess. My judgment is that he was probably a teenager, fourteen, fifteen, something like that. Nor do we know what year this was. It may have been a couple of years after Jesus, which would put it about 37 or 38. Maybe later.

A few verses later in Acts 12, we encounter John Mark again. Paul had been converted to Christianity—you remember the Damascas Road story—and was in Antioch, up north from Jerusalem. One of the leaders of the Antioch church was a man named Barnabas, by all indications a wealthy man, very generous, well loved, and respected in the church, both in Jerusalem and Antioch. Barnabas befriended Saul—he was Saul then—and when Barnabas was asked to take money from the Antioch church to the Jerusalem church, he asked Saul to go with him. He would vouch for Saul there, since Saul was certainly not trusted in Jerusalem. Before his conversion, remember, he had created havoc for the church. Chapter 12 says that after Barnabas and Saul completed their mission, they returned to Antioch, but, the text says, they took John—"whose other name was Mark"—with them.

The next thing we know, at the beginning of chapter 13 of Acts, is that Barnabas and Saul are commissioned—that's a good word for it—to go on a trip to begin new churches. They sail for Cyprus, that long island out there in the Mediterranean, the place, incidentally, where Barnabas was from. Then we are told that the two of them took with them—

yes—John Mark. He was to be what the Greek text calls their "helper," their "assistant." After a time in Cyprus, they headed north, back to the mainland. Their first stop on the coast is the city of Perga in Pamphylia. There, as Barnabas and Saul begin their work, there is an ominous, though seemingly innocuous, note in the text. It says, and I will quote it, "John, however, left them and returned to Jerusalem."

Barnabas and Saul continue on their trip, ending up back in Antioch, their home base. Other things transpire, particularly in Jerusalem. Then, toward the end of Acts 15, we are told that someone—I think it was Paul (Saul was now called Paul)—suggested that he and Barnabas return to the churches they had started on their first trip to see how they were doing and give them a boost. Barnabas agreed. Then, matter-of-factly, I think, Barnabas told Paul that John Mark wanted to go with them again. Paul's response was fairly direct: "Not on your life. He left us the first time and we don't need that again."

Barnabas agreed, I think, but urged Paul, saying that John Mark—who, by the way, was Barnabas's cousin—"John Mark has changed a good deal since then; he'll do fine with us this time."

Paul said something pretty plain, like "Over my dead body he will." That's a rough, but very accurate translation of the Greek. Then—seriously—we are told that the two of them had what the Greek text calls a "sharp contention," a heated, bitter, very close to violent, argument. Hard to believe, but true. And all over John Mark's now disastrous decision to return home on the first trip. Paul called it desertion. It appears to have come to the point where Barnabas said something like, "If John Mark doesn't go, then I don't go." Paul's response was "If that's the way you want it, so be it." And these two very close friends—Paul owed Barnabas everything—these two broke up. Over John Mark. The text says that Barnabas took John Mark and they sailed for Cyprus. And we have no idea what they did after that. Paul selected a new partner, named Silas, and the two of them, along with some others, sailed off to where they had gone before. The story of Acts follows Paul and Silas.

Wow! Can you imagine? Can you sense the depth of anger and bitterness, all because of John Mark—this grief between Paul and Barnabas? When you think about it, it is almost unimaginable. We can date the event somewhat. Most scholars tell us that the first trip that Paul and Barnabas took, the one where John Mark left them, was probably between 45 to 48. If John Mark was a teenager in the late 30s, when Peter was released from prison, then he is now in his mid-twenties or a little older. The second trip, the one that Paul went on without Barnabas, probably began in about 49 or 50. So John Mark could well be about twenty-seven or twenty-eight at this point. It's a guess.

Then years pass. Ten years or so probably pass. We can reasonably set the next date at 60 or 61, sometime along in there, which would make John Mark now approaching forty. Paul's trips are over, and he is in prison in Rome, perhaps under house arrest, but a prisoner, nonetheless. Paul writes from prison. He writes two letters that we have and that appear to have been written at almost the same time. One is his letter to the church in Colossae, our Colossians; and the other is a short personal letter to a man named Philemon, a man whom Paul may have never met, but he knew him by reputation for his Christian character. He says so in the letter. Paul had somehow met Philemon's runaway slave, whose name was Onesimus. You probably know the story—we have in our New Testament a little one-chapter letter called Philemon: Paul sent Onesimus back to Philemon with that brief letter.

The point is this, though. At the end of both of those letters is a stunning line. Something totally unexpected. At the end of Colossians, the line says this. Listen. "Aristarchus my fellow prisoner greets you, as does Mark the cousin of Barnabas." As does Mark, the cousin of Barnabas. Mark has suddenly reappeared. Not till here. There is another line right after that one in Colossians, though, that is utterly intriguing. It reads—you can look it up—it reads: "You have received instructions—if he comes to you, welcome him." Did you hear that? Did you hear that? What instructions? Paul says whatever you have heard about Mark, it is in the past. What they heard about John Mark they probably heard from Paul. And now Paul says, forget it. When Mark comes to you, welcome him. I don't know about you, but, for me, that is one of the more remarkable lines in all of Paul's writing.

At the end of the little letter to Philemon, written at the same time I think, is this line: "Epaphras, my fellow prisoner in Christ Jesus, sends greetings to you, so [does] Mark. . . ." And so does Mark. No explanations. Just a warm greeting from Mark, passed along by Paul.

There is one other reference to Mark worth noting, though we are much less clear about who wrote it. It is in 2 Timothy, chapter 4, verse 11. It is attributed to Paul, but most likely was written by someone close to Paul, perhaps someone who wrote down things he heard Paul say before his death. It's hard to tell. At any rate, the reference is extraordinarily warm. The line, addressed to Timothy, says this. Listen. "Get Mark and bring him with you, for he is useful in my ministry." Get Mark and bring him with you, for he is useful in my ministry.

More than ten years, at least, passed between the breakup of Paul and Barnabas over John Mark and the writing of these notes by Paul about John Mark. "Mark sends greetings. Get John Mark and bring him with you, because I need him." What happened during that long ten-year stretch? Something changed. Our minds can only guess. Did Paul realize how harsh he had been about John Mark back there in Antioch? This is the Paul who wrote in 1 Corinthians 13, the love chapter, that love is not . . . "provoked"—the very same Greek word that Acts uses to describe Paul's action toward Mark. Did Paul realize what he had done to Mark? Did he write to Mark and ask him to come see him? Or did John Mark realize what a mistake he had made in his youth, and did he write a letter to Paul, apologizing and asking for another chance, the chance

he did not get back then? At any rate, at the end of Paul's life—
Paul was probably martyred in about 64 or 65 under Nero—
Mark was there with him, perhaps till the end.

But the story is not over. There is a remarkable final chapter to it. After Paul's death, between 65 and 70 of that first century, the Romans seem to have gone on a rampage. They went
in all directions, but one of the places that they seem to have
concentrated on was the little country of Palestine, home of
both Jews and Christians, the place where Pilate and Herod
had overseen the crucifixion of the one called Jesus. The
Roman army occupied the country and proceeded to destroy
it. The date that historians put on the destruction of Jerusalem
and the Jewish Temple is 70. Jews were massacred. Christians,
for the most part, had dispersed—as had many Jews, of
course. But because the country and its capital city were being
destroyed, some scholars believe—I think rightly—that there
was a need for someone, someone to pull together what had
been a lot of diverse writings, stories, traditions, letters, and so
forth about Jesus and his life in that very area. Materials did
exist, but they were scattered.

What Christian tradition tells us is that one person stepped
up. One person understood the need: a man by then going on
about fifty years of age, a seasoned veteran of Christianity; he
probably sealed himself up in a small study someplace—not in
Jerusalem, but perhaps in Antioch or someplace like that. He
had with him a lot of parchments, collections of Jesus' teachings and sayings, statements about what Jesus did and what
happened to him, and copies of a lot of Paul's letters, Paul's
theological writing. This man arranged everything on the desk
and, in the course of a week or so—if I may speculate—he
wrote a short story of Jesus. That man's name was John Mark,
and what he produced in the heat of that turbulent time was
our Gospel of Mark. It was the first of our Gospels; the Gospel
on which our other Gospels—Matthew, Luke, and even
John—were based. It was Mark who rose to that remarkable
occasion—the very same Mark who deserted Paul early in his

life, who caused Paul such enormous pain that it split up the great Paul and Barnabas team. This was the Mark who, after what appears to have been a long agony over his separation from Paul, came back from it to write the gospel of Jesus Christ. It was this Mark who sat down, probably alone, and wrote his Gospel, and the world was never the same again!

That's the story of John Mark. It is an amazing story. If we—excuse me, I have to catch my breath. If we think back over the course of Mark's life, tracing its eras or decades, as in 28 Up, what are we to say about it? We can celebrate it, of course, but we need to do more than that. Let me see if we can focus a bit. John Mark went through a terrible ordeal. It was very public in the churches—remember that the Colossians were told to pay no attention to what they had heard about John Mark. An ordeal of his own making, for the most part. But it was a public humiliation, if there ever was one—again that line from Colossians gives it away. Still, even though it took a long time, Mark not only recovered from it, he not only came back from it, but he came back in the end to write a Christian Gospel that would change the world. John Mark made a lot of mistakes—painful mistakes—not only painful to himself but to a lot of people around him, people who trusted him. But he came back. He overcame, and out of his experience he wrote—listen to this—he wrote the First Gospel.

Bottom line? You and I can take heart from John Mark. We can learn from him. If he could come back from failures, from painful mistakes, whatever one might want to call them, if he could come back from them, live through the humiliation, face up to what he had done, be reconciled to Paul and others whom he had hurt, and, out of it all, create a Gospel, then so can I; so can you.

One of the people I admire these days is a young woman—she is still young, I have known her for quite a long time—a young woman whom I shall call Jennie. She was a teenager when I first met her, living with her grandmother and grandfather; her mother had given her up for a life of drugs. But

Jennie was a wild one; not just typical wild, but far-out-on-the-edge wild. She knew drugs, but because of what she watched her mother turn into, she was somewhat afraid of drugs. But she was wild in other ways. Mostly with her boyfriends. She was pregnant when I met her. She would come to church occasionally with her grandparents, bringing her new son, who was growing up very fast. I got acquainted with her. She would talk with me occasionally, even calling me now and then as her minister when something went bad, which it often did for her.

I was driving that afternoon when I heard the news story on the car radio. A bank in our town had been held up by a young man and young woman; he did the holdup and she drove the getaway car. Both of them had been caught on remote bank cameras. Police were looking for them—and they had their names already. The boy's name I did not know, but I sure knew hers. I cried. I thought maybe I'd get a call, but I didn't. Instead, I went to see her grandparents, who were taking care of the baby—their great-grandson. We cried together. Jennie had been gone for more than a week, and they had no idea where she was. They saw it all on the TV news that evening. The next morning's newspaper told the story. Jennie and her boyfriend had been caught that night and arrested. It was two days before I could see her, and over the next months we talked occasionally, and I attended part of her trial—he got seven years in state prison and she got five. It was up north, but she wrote a couple of times, and I wrote back.

After two and a half years, she got out. She moved back, got reacquainted with her almost five-year-old son; he was still with her grandparents. They managed to put aside their grief and anger and take her back. The question was whether she could or would turn things around. She had been front-page news during her arrest and trial, and every place she went after she got back, people remembered her. Then, something happened, and Jennie started working hard on her life. She faced up to what she had done. She changed. Her grandparents, who did not have very much, scrimped to send her to cosmetology school. In time, she met a good young man, and after a year and a half they had a daughter. Jennie and her family found the company of the church again. I watched. I saw. She grew up, and she did so in a way that not only learned from her past, but that wanted to help other young women not fall into what she did. Jennie came back from an experience that very few of us can imagine. She came back and began—can I say it this way?—she came back and began to write a gospel, her gospel.

We all know to some degree the Mark experience, the Jennie experience. Though ours is not exactly parallel, we know it. Remember we began by thinking back over the decades of our own lives. We all know those desertions, those failures, those things that we wish we had not done—that if we had not done, we would not have caused so much grief and pain to ourselves and people around us. Is there anyone here who has no idea what we're talking about?

Mark was not old when he wrote his Gospel, but he was not young either. He wrote his Gospel in midlife. Jennie's gospel, written small not large, but a gospel nevertheless, is getting an earlier start. I know some who have begun writing a gospel at age eighty and above. The point is that no matter how old you are, no matter how old I am, we are never too old to start writing a gospel. We can start now. Everything else has been preparation for writing our gospel. I think that was the case with John Mark. I seriously doubt if John Mark could have written the Gospel that he did without the long years of painful preparation. No matter what you have done, have lived through, or are still trying to survive, you can write your own gospel.

How does one write a gospel today? Sure, we are not going to do like Mark did, quill and parchment in hand at the table. But we can think about it figuratively, as I have done with Jennie. Let me make a few suggestions.

We write gospels today by the ways in which we conduct our lives. In a time of what the great American humorist Garrison Keillor has called "elephantine vanity and greed," we can live lives of gentle humility and generosity, lives of unbroken kindness and courtesy. Loving people, even—or particularly—strangers, is not some big thing, not some great, large act that one does. Loving people wherever and however we rub shoulders with them in a thousand little things; it is the "please" and "thank you" we supposedly were taught as children, but have long since forgotten. It is the courtesy of a smile or a friendly word to someone who is upset. It is a gentle, friendly wave at someone who has cut us off on the freeway. When our lives are made of these patterns of living, we are writing a gospel for our own time.

Another suggestion. We write gospels today by how we handle our resources. There is greed and mad accumulation of money everywhere. To be generous, to know that it is better to give than to receive, to practice the Christian art of sharing what we have, expecting nothing in return, with those who have so little, with poor parents and children in our communities, in our cities. There are ways to do this, if we search them out. If there are not ways to do it where you are, then create some. In doing that, you will be writing a very important gospel.

One more. It is my belief that one writes a gospel today also by being a visible, physical presence in a community of Christian faith. Can one be a Christian and not go to church? Of course—who am I to say that that is not possible? But—but—Christian community enriches not only your own life, but the lives of all those who, with you, allow themselves to become bonded to one another. What richness of texture and meaning in life one finds and one gives to others. What a sense of togetherness, of never facing anything alone. One both gives and receives from such a community. Churches write gospels today, too; at least they can and ought to. And I know a lot of them that do. Groups of people, bound and working together, can do more in a community than any single individual can ever accomplish alone. One writes a gospel with one's life by becoming committed to such a divine community.

We can still write gospels today—you and I. John Mark came back from a difficult life of desertion, rejection, loneliness—who knows what—but he came back to write a Gospel that changed the world. Gospels are still needed. Needed in a thousand places and ways. You can write one of those gospels, as only you can. Will you? Shall we begin?

Notes

Introduction: Why Preach Without Script or Notes?

1. John A. Broadus, *A Treatise on the Preparation and Delivery of Sermons* (New York: A. C. Armstrong and Son, 1899). Between 1870 and 1899, the book had gone though thirty-seven printings, and that number multiplied throughout the twentieth century. Remarkably, one reading Broadus today is still likely to find some of the most helpful and thorough instruction in the fine points of sermon development and presentation. This edition was edited after Broadus's death by Edwin Charles Dargan, himself an eminent homiletician and historian of preaching.

2. Ibid., 439-40.

3. Ibid., 444.

4. Ibid., 468.

5. Ibid.

6. Ibid., 462.

7. Ibid., 463-64.

8. See the summary report, *Agenda 21: United Methodist Ministry for a New Century*. A Project of the Association of United Methodist Theological Schools, October 1995, section 3.

9. In 1946, Clarence Edward Macartney, in a book called *Preaching Without Notes* (New York: Abingdon-Cokesbury Press) wrote: "In season and out of season, year after year, and to the average congregation, there can be no question that the sermon that does the most good is the sermon which is preached without notes" (145).

A decade after that, in 1956, Ilion T. Jones, in another book from Abingdon Press entitled *Principles and Practice of Preaching*, wrote that "every time laymen are given a chance to express themselves they vote against the reading of sermons" (194-95).

And, Charles W. Koller, in the book, *Expository Preaching Without Notes* (Grand Rapids: Baker Book House, 1962), to which reference was made earlier, wrote: "There are, as there always have been, ministers who preach effectively from manuscript or copious notes in the pulpit ... but the same preachers would be even more effective if they could stand note free in the pulpit. This seems clearly to be the verdict of history" (34).

133

Chapter One: Planning the Sermon Without Notes: Monday and Tuesday

1. There are numerous books that explore the preacher's relationship to the Bible and its texts, too many to try to list here. One will find my own discussion of these larger issues in my book, *Old Texts, New Sermons: The Quiet Revolution in Biblical Preaching* (St. Louis: Chalice Press, 2000).

2. See, for example, Joseph M. Webb, *Comedy and Preaching* (St. Louis: Chalice Press, 1998).

Chapter Two: Creating the Sermon Outline: Wednesday

1. Charles W. Koller, *Expository Preaching Without Notes* (Grand Rapids: Baker Book House, 1962). This sermon is found on pages 96 and 97.

Chapter Three: Memorizing the Sermon Outline: Thursday and Friday

1. Any good library will have a number of books, many of them recent, on the research into memory. One of the best that I have found is by Eugene B. Zechmeister and Stanley E. Nyberg, *Human Memory: An Introduction to Research and Theory* (Monterey, Calif.: Brooks-Cole Publishing Company, 1982). Among other books that would prove useful to the preacher are D. Herrmann, D. Raybeck, and D. Gutman, *Improving Student Memory* (Seattle: Hogrefe & Huber Publishers, 1993), and John G. Seamon, *Memory and Cognition: An Introduction* (New York: Oxford University Press, 1980).

2. See Zechmeister and Nyberg, 43.

Chapter Four: Delivering the Sermon Without Notes: Sunday

1. John A. Broadus, *A Treatise on the Preparation and Delivery of Sermons* (New York: A.C. Armstrong and Son, 1899), 459.